MW00625263

THE POWER
of
PEACE
in a
P A U S E

TIERRA DESTINY REID

TDR Brands Publishing
Atlanta

Congratulations isha!!! Happy Holidays Tierra Desty

www.tierradestinyreid.com

Excerpt from *A Return to Love* by Marianne Williamson. Copyright © 1992 by Marianne Williamson. Reprinted by permission of Marianne Williamson.
Quotation used by permission of Martha Beck.

Book designed by Britney R. LaRoche
Book reviewed and edited by Prasanna Ranganathan
Book transcribed by Marie Sanjurjo
Cover designed by Kaye Homecillo
Cover photo by Rich Cruse
Edited by Britney R. LaRoche

The Library of Congress Cataloging-in-Publication Data is available upon request.

ISBN 978-0-9907516-0-1 (paperback)

First Edition: October 2014

ACKNOWLEDGEMENTS

I would like to thank God for placing this book and the lessons within me. I am grateful for the obedience, support, and strength it took to complete it.

I'm thankful for my husband and children who have shared the most intimate parts of this chapter on my journey. They are forever in my heart. A special thanks to all the family and friends who have contributed to making this work a success: Editor Britney LaRoche, for your humble spirit guiding me along without pressure or judgment; Myia, for being a soft place to fall and a voice of reason; Mom, for reminding me to live without limits and do what's best for me, not everyone else; Bina, for your commitment to growth; Lorea Sample and Felicia Joy for being obedient and embracing your journeys; Prasanna, for caring enough to support and share your wisdom; Oprah Winfrey and team, for taking the hard hits and sharing the tools that I actively used during this chapter of awakening; Martha Beck, for your words of wisdom and allowing them to be shared; OWN Ambassadors, for being love and light; Connie Gilbert, for your quiet strength. I'm rooting for you; Ericka Thomas, for your honesty, excellence, and loyalty; Leroy, for your loyalty and love; Lemuel LaRoche, for leading by example; Marsheila Parrish, for pushing me forward when I wanted to fall back; Angela Stalcup, for writing the foreword and your continued support; Amandeep, for your gentle strength, open heart, and our tea time together in Chicago. I'll never forget our talk. I'm waiting on you next; my former Macy's family, for training me to survive in any business setting and supporting my entrepreneurial journey after the layoff; Tory and the world of Daring Doers, for showing me that dreams are possible and reminding me that this was a luxury and not an opportunity most women can take; and last, but not least, I would like to thank the women who were brave enough to share their stories with me to help liberate others.

What started off as simple journaling to cleanse my spirit has been birthed into a book. Wow! Who knew?

DEDICATION

I would like to dedicate this book to the doers, fixers, and builders; the ones who are always there for others, serving, giving, and leading. Those of us on the frontline, whether we are entrepreneurs, community leaders, or homemakers, often need moments to pause the most. Those moments allow us to refuel for the next chapter, just as a marathon runner has seasons of rest and training before the next race. Tap into the power of your full potential with a pause. It truly transformed my life and has propelled me forward mentally, spiritually, and physically. You deserve to live on full. Take the time to refuel.

I would also like to dedicate this book to all of those before me who sacrificed their lives and dreams, and to those after me. This is my leg of the race to run in your honor. Pausing when my spirit tells me to is how I plan to pass the torch.

With Love,

Tierra Destiny

FOREWORD

written by
Angela Stalcup

It all started with the tights.

I was at an event for women entrepreneurs, wearing my black-sculpted, Eiffel Tower tights, when this bright-eyed, energetic woman approached me and said, "These tights — this is you. This should represent your brand!" And knowing nothing else about this woman, I knew she had spirit and vision. Only later would I learn the power behind that spirit.

As an advocate for women entrepreneurs, I've worked with over a thousand women in the last seven years, and I've seen a pattern emerge. First, there are the dreamers who never do — the people with big ideas, big visions, who plan and study and research, but never act to make the dream a reality. Then there are the doers that never dream — they are constantly in action, changing tactics on a daily basis, mistaking busy-ness with business, and they dream about doing things a new way.

However, there's a third category, the category of women that I know will succeed — the dreamers that do. These are the people who go from vision to action, those who capture the vision, wrangle it into actionable chunks, and act at the time that is right for them. It didn't take me long to figure out that Tierra is in the *dreamers that do* category, and when she "does," she acts in a big way.

I was fortunate enough to meet Tierra early in her entrepreneurial career. It was the end of 2009, and she had opened her first retail store (on a shoestring budget) and was just launching her networking and educational events. Watching Tierra in action, it became clear to me that she knew how to partner vision with action. Everything she touched, from the signage in the store to the layouts of displays, to the gift bags at events, showed attention to detail no matter how small. More impressively, she brought her passion and enthusiasm to the people around her, be they customers in the store, attendees at an event, or guest speakers. She backed up all of this with a deep knowledge of business and marketing, and the store prospered and grew.

As I attended events at Tierra's store, I could see something bigger growing, a movement, with Tierra at the center. What many coaches and experts tried to build was forming naturally around Tierra—a community. Women began seeking Tierra out for advice, for mentoring. They wanted to be like her, to learn the secret of her success. Tierra was just trying to have a successful retail space and to drive customer engagement with events, but I, and others around her, could see that it was so much more.

Her middle name is *Destiny* — it should have been obvious that she was bound for big things.

The vision was so clear to me that I had to share it with her. Or perhaps more accurately, I just needed to hold up what I like to call *the loving mirror* and show her the potential. I told her, "I can see that you are a doer. The vision is clear. I know you'll do it." And she did it.

All she needed was a little structure around her mentoring and business advice, and boom, it exploded. From the outside looking in, it appeared effortless. She produced a series of conferences, became a nationally recognized speaker, and began working as a mentor to other women with the dream of entrepreneurship.

And the story could end here — her retail business boomed, her consulting business took off like a wildfire, and Tierra could be working night and day serving the needs of two businesses. Success! Roll credits. Turn up the houselights.

But that's not how the story ends.

In the midst of all of this energy and movement, Tierra stepped on the brakes. Tierra pressed pause.

This isn't what we're told to do. We're told to "make hay while the sun shines," to "hit the ground running and never look back." And that's what lots of us do. We struggle and sweat to bring a dream to life, then we let that dream drag us wherever it wants to go. We forget what Tierra realized—we drive the dream, the dream doesn't drive us.

The power of the pause is profound for a business. The process of vision to action isn't a straight line—it's cyclical. We begin with vision, we plan and clarify, we act, then we must review. Re-vision. Re-act. It's an ongoing, never-ending process. Without a pause, there is no space for the adaptation and growth.

I've asked many successful women this question: *How did you know when to stop planning and start doing, when to let the purpose unfold in the action?* And they all have given me the same basic answer—intuition. They describe a feeling, a sense, an inclination that pushed them to go from planning to action. It's Tierra, however, who has provided the piece that I rarely hear described—how to connect with intuition, how to hear what your *gut* is telling you. You truly hear in the pause.

And while the pause is important in business, even more importantly, the power of the pause is profound for life. That same intuition that is giving you guidance on launching and running a business is giving you clues about launching and running your life. We dream of passion-filled lives, but passion must meet purpose to become real and tangible. The pause is the key to creating purposeful passion in any and all areas of our lives.

And that's Tierra—purposeful, passionate, positive. She's lived the advice she's giving here. She's had multiple successful businesses, she's had the courage to take a pause, and she has returned to the momentum with renewed vigor and focus. Now there's a success story.

In this book, you will find your own success story, whatever it looks like, by learning the power of peace in a pause. To quote Glinda the Good Witch, when it comes to your purposeful passionate life, "You've always had it, my dear." And to quote Tierra Destiny Reid, "You'll find it in the pause."

Angela Stalcup is a small business development expert and an advocate for female entrepreneurship. She is the CEO of Angela Stalcup Group, LLC, a strategic communications consulting firm started in 1994. Angela is passionate about helping women live their best lives and she has worked as an entrepreneurial advocate through organizations such as Ladies Who Launch, Girltank, and the APEX Enrichment Institute. She also works as a body-image advocate through her blog, The Curvy Life. An in-demand speaker and author, Angela has been featured in national print, radio, and television media. Learn more about Angela at www.AngelaStalcup.com.

CONTENTS

Part III: You're in the Pause. Now What?

... Some of the most beautiful art has nothing to do with the colors at all, but rather the heart and passion displayed by the artist. We are all artists, with the chance to paint our own picture ...

-*Tierra Destiny*

INTRODUCTION

Peace is one of the most powerful states of being that any human can accept. Inner peace is what allows a person to stand in the midst of a tragedy or chaos and remain unbroken. There is power in knowing that outer circumstances don't have to control your inner reality.

There are over seven billion people on Earth. Imagine all of us being given the same news. We would all process it differently, with various thoughts and emotions triggering our response. Some would crumble, while some would be unmoved. But there would also be a special group of people who have an ability to accept the situation, accept their emotions while remaining open and vulnerable, and still stand from their inner core with peace of mind, knowing that all things work together and don't have to determine their entire reality.

Living in a reactive state will keep us in constant motion. Let's face it, life happens. But will you be in a whirlwind every time you get upsetting news? Will you be up and down depending upon what everyone around you says or does? Are you bold enough to pause and accept your ultimate power within? Through *The Power of Peace in a Pause,* I hope you will find yourself awakened and rejuvenated in your ability to ask the tough questions and face the honest answers.

Believe it or not, I started journaling about my pause roughly two years ago and as I sat down to edit the book you are holding in your hand, I realized how hard it is to face some of the situations that life brings our way. It's easy to say we are bold and honest, but hard to truly embrace those things that may shift our entire reality. In this book I will discuss the power of a pause and how the peace you'll have will elevate you to a new level of experiences on your journey.

Before we go any further, I want to be very clear and upfront. I am not a psychologist, professor, or expert who proclaims to know exactly why you need to pause or how you should live your life. Life is tough and everyone's journey is completely different. I am an everyday woman with a family, hopes, and dreams just like you. I am very committed to self-improvement and becoming the best person I can be. I love sharing information and connecting with amazing people. After becoming a national speaker, I found that most women were seeking many of the same things, but perhaps, in different forms; thus, leading me to write down my thoughts on this topic.

What makes this process interesting is that up until

my shift began, I was always in constant motion. I typically have several projects going on at once. If you had told me that I would actually sit still and embrace time for reflection, literally dedicating two years of my life to become my own project, I would have looked at you like you had three heads. Before then, I took on the philosophy that time was to be used. Every second of it was pertinent to building our dreams and leading us to find our purpose.

After pausing I realized that time to learn and embrace who we are after many life lessons, was time well spent. This allows us to be present in the world as we truly are, and not how others perceive us to be.

That's what makes this chapter of my journey so intense. I was never still long enough to finish a twenty-page paper, let alone an entire book. This wasn't even my initial plan, but through obedience, lots of reconditioning, a solid support system, and getting brutally honest with myself, we are finally here, together. You and I.

You are reading a book that blossomed out of real life experiences captured on paper by me and a few amazing women who I admire for being open and brave enough to pause and share. They also transformed through their pauses, which allowed them to overcome rejection, failure, fear of success, infidelity, heartbreak, and knowing when to let go.

The book is broken down into three parts:

1. Are You Bold Enough to Pause?

2. It's Possible: Real Women Share Their Pauses

3. You're in the Pause. Now What?

In Part One, you will discover what it truly means to pause and begin tackling some of the things that may be hindering you from doing so.

Next, you'll read real life accounts from women who have been where you are. Enjoy their stories as they share their experiences and insight on how pausing transformed their lives.

And finally, we close with Part Three where we will explore what to expect once you've decided to pause.

After reading *The Power of Peace in a Pause* you will:
- *Expand your inner peace and confidence*
- *Have a better understanding of your gifts and who you are*
- *Be more equipped to serve and build*
- *Become more resilient in your quest to live out your dreams*
- *Embrace and dedicate future chapters of your journey to pausing, reflecting, and preparing for your next climb*

- *Recognize and pay closer attention to signs that you may have overlooked in the past*

My wish is that you will gain more insight about yourself, your truth, your brilliance, and ultimately your power. Changing the world around you begins with embracing all that you are. Your voice, your heart, your mind; they all matter. You are powerful and perfectly created to serve your purpose in this world. Let's embrace our power with peace so that we can hear what is being spoken within our spirit and waiting to guide us on the next path in our journey.

◆ ◆ ◆

"Everyone is racing to the Next Thing.

Well, I got caught up in that for a really long time — so much so, that I could never really enjoy what I WAS doing, because I was always worried about what I was going to be doing.

I tell you all this, because I know right now everybody's asking you those same questions: "What are you gonna do after graduation? Do you have a job? Where will you be working? How much are they paying? Where are you going? Where will you be living? Who are you seeing?" Oh, my God — so many questions!

And here you are: sitting there ready to hit the Fast Forward button and find out the answers. I get that. I was just LIKE you: I lived on Fast Forward.

But today, I have one wish for you. Before you go out and press that fast forward button, I'm hoping - I'm praying - that you'll have the courage to first press the pause button.

That's right: the pause button. I hope if you learn anything from me today, you learn and remember — The Power of the Pause."[1]

-Maria Shriver

---

[1] Shriver, Maria. "The Power of the Pause." *Maria Shriver-Powered by Inspiration.*

PART I

Are You Bold Enough To Pause?

I once raved about being a *strong* woman. Now I look in the mirror and see a *brave* woman. Thankful that I'm wise enough to now understand the difference. I want this feeling for others.

-*Tierra Destiny*

ONE

It's Your Time: Start Tapping the Breaks

Life gets crazy. Life is busy. We are pulled in a million directions. The emails are constant. The kids need love and attention. Projects pile up. Dreams are deferred, and before we know it, one year is flowing into the next.

Have you ever felt like you were running fast, only to end up in the same place? Or do you feel like I did? Working hard, making progress, but barely scratching the surface of your potential and your vision? If so, then pause. Yes. Stop and get still. Get silent and get real. Real honest. Something is off. Out of alignment, out of place, not flowing. We are not here to just get it done. We want to make sure we are doing what we are *supposed* to be doing, which leads us to the fulfillment we are looking for.

I remember looking out of the window in Washington, D.C. I had just completed my fourth *Design Your Destiny Conference For Women*. I will never forget the feeling of fulfillment I had, while also feeling like I was cheating myself. I knew I was doing the right thing, but perhaps, not the right way. Many questions raced through my mind: Am I going fast enough? Will we gain the support we need to take this vision beyond where it is? Will I always feel tired afterwards? Is it supposed to be this way? What is it that I am seeking? If I am helping so many people and doing something I love, why do I feel like there is so much more?

Because there is. There is more. More we must learn about ourselves, our limitations, our areas of opportunity, our true desires, our true intent, and we must do the work.

I realized that during my pause, there was so much work to do and so many layers to uncover that I would literally have to sit at a table, dump out everything I had learned, sort through it, de-clutter, and keep what was healthy and served my calling. What began as a pause became a personal sabbatical and journey within.

"In life, there are some things you cannot work your way to, but you must work your way through!"

One day a girlfriend and I had lunch and she shared how her days were so packed with everything for everyone else— her kids, her husband, her church— that there was no time left for herself. After juicing, preparing healthy meals from scratch, and making sure that the kids had amazing educational reinforcement, there were simply no more hours in the day. "There's no time for me," she said. "I haven't had a manicure, vacation, or bubble bath in I don't know how long."

I looked at her and told her that I knew exactly how she felt because I had experienced being totally present for my children and household to take care of the *so-called* right things for my family. But somehow there were days that I would end up just as tired as when I was running my storefront. I was literally left exhausted because my favorite things were nowhere on my to-do list.

She expressed that she had her children on a set schedule, but still found it difficult to tell me what she accomplished during the week. There was no real structure and no time blocked out for the things she loved most. Again, I could relate because somehow it was easy to catch up on all the other things going on in my life while unconsciously forgetting about myself. Even simply spending a few minutes each day exercising would have helped to decrease tension and allowed me to begin focusing on those things necessary for my personal growth.[2]

Sometimes we think we are being responsible and doing the right thing by striving for the best for our families and others, but are neglecting the joys of experiencing our life at its highest potential.

Have you ever wondered what it would feel like to become your own priority? What if you had time to just focus on understanding yourself from the inside out and committed to slowing down and stopping all the unnecessary actions in your life to get still?

Today that seems almost unheard of. People often share with me that they've taken a week or two off, but have they truly used that time to pause?

Before we begin, let's define *pause*:

1. a temporary stop
2. a break in a verse
3. temporary inaction especially as caused by uncertainty

Synonyms
break, breath, breather, interruption, lull, recess

---

[2] "Exercise for Stress and Anxiety." *Anxiety and Depression Association of America*. Web. <http://www.adaa.org/living-with-anxiety/managing-anxiety/exercise-stress-and-anxiety>.

For the purpose of this book, we will define a conscious *pause* as **a bold and continuous period of limited outside interaction to commit to internal reflection and determine the right action to take or not to take to align with your purpose and destiny.** In other words, we are shutting out the noise and clearing out the debris.

During this period your mind can settle a bit, allowing you to focus on a clearer image. Many of us fall into *regulated norms*, which neither allow us a moment to breathe nor produce outcomes at our *maximum* potential.

Imagine being on a road trip with someone who's driving beyond the speed limit. You may notice the beautiful skyline and trees, completely appreciating the greenery and the wind blowing on your face, but miss the signs along the way that say *STOP HERE FOR A FREE CUP OF COFFEE* or *FROM 2:00-3:00 P.M., ANYONE DRIVING ON THIS ROAD EARNS A FREE GAS CARD.* Now imagine the driver slowing down for you to really take in the view. How much more are you bound to see? There are things we notice and things we don't depending upon:

- **Speed**– The pace at which we move about our day
- **Focus**– What we put emphasis on in our lives
- **Conversations**– What we talk about
- **Thoughts**– The things we allow to fill our minds

- **Company**– Who we surround ourselves with
- **Deadlines**– The time limits set before us

Speed

Speed not only refers to how fast you are going, but also the structure and process in which things are flowing. Operating at high speeds without structure can be detrimental.

Believe it or not, I've been there at various points on my journey. Even highly ambitious people can sometimes find themselves in *just get it done* mode without the right guardrails. I laugh as I remember literally standing in the living room telling my husband that I felt like a pro baseball player sometimes. I envisioned myself standing at the batting cage constantly in practice, steadily swinging at every ball thrown my way, until I trained so hard that my productivity increased and my work ethic and technique were refined. The only objection to this is that everything must be done in moderation. I now also understand that some conversations and opportunities are not even worth swinging at or responding to.

Focus

Focus means to pay attention. A pause will require focus so that you can get still to see a clear picture of the things that are in front of you.

When you shake a snow globe, what do you see? Lots of snow floating around a beautiful image inside. Now sit it down for a moment. Without the constant motion, it only took one minute for the picture to become clearer. The same picture you have been living in can become very clear with just a little time to pause. Until now you didn't notice there was a sign on the little door in the globe that had your name on it. You just thought it was a generic gift your coworker picked up. You assumed she just grabbed something in her haste to be nice. After closer examination, you realize that the mat also has *I ♥ATL* on it because she knows how much you miss being there. Without focusing or paying attention, we miss some really special signs that could add to our present experience.

Conversations and Thoughts

Think about being with someone for eight hours. You will most likely talk about a variety of topics. Whether you agree with the other person or not, you hear what they are saying and you process it. Most of us operate on this level quite often, paying little attention to who we are talking to and what we are speaking about. This is critical because, as we know, when things are spoken into the atmosphere and taken in, they enter our thoughts. We process them, and even if we disagree, they could potentially influence our perspective.

Your view or level of admiration for the person you are speaking with may determine the level of influence their perspective has on you. You may end up veering off in a direction that you were never intending to go. But due to the power of influence, admiration, and thoughts, you are now processing new information. In the sales industry millions of dollars are invested in training consultants on the topic of persuasion and seed planting. Do your research. The mind is powerful and we must pay attention to what we are processing.

A pause will allow you time to process welcomed information and become aware of the direction you are going in. This may seem like very basic knowledge, but think about how much information we process in a day with a full to-do list and deadlines. We are often forced by the way of the world to think quickly. This comes naturally for some, but many people will simply *go with the flow*. Ask yourself if you are the type to go along with the current or are your brave, bold, and self-aware enough to pause. *Think, decide, and then act.*

Company

The company you keep influences the thoughts you process, which become your reality. Let's pause for a moment.

16

Pause #1

List your five most common relationships and the three topics you typically discuss. Here's my list:

People	Topics
Husband	Future, Finances, Kids
Sister	Business, Relationships, Parents
Best Friend	Marriage, Kids, Goals
Best Friend	Relationships, Kids, Goals
Co-Worker	Business, Goals, Growth

Those conversations, their experiences, and your experience impact your thoughts, which will impact your decisions.

The company you keep impacts your direction, progression or regression in life. Choose your company carefully. Stopping to decide how you want your life to be may give you the time to assess the quality of the relationships in your life. You can determine if they are truly a fit for where you want to be or if they're stuck where you have been.

Some people in your life only do well when they *complete* you. Pay attention. There are some people that we lean on when we are still broken to feel more comfortable. But we must do the work to grow into who we want to become. This is why pausing to decide and envision it is so important. After a few years of growing, you must check in with yourself to see who you are now, today, with all of life's experiences. Now from here, where do you want to go? Who will you become? I recently heard Bishop T.D. Jakes say, "Press the reset button!"[3]

Deadlines and Goals

Deadlines and goals help us progress in the direction we initially set out on. It is important to consider a few things:

- Deadlines can put a great amount of pressure on us and have us in constant motion
- Deadlines are great when we are in complete alignment with our purpose because they fuel action
- Deadlines keep us accountable
- Often deadlines create laser focus, however, we may also miss other signs that we are not aware of or surpass

Having tunnel vision has helped me reach several goals in record time; however, I had to open up and realize that there are typically other options as well. Looking at things from a panoramic view can sometimes help you achieve goals without

---

[3] "How to Hit the Reset Button After Losing Your Dream Job - Oprah's Lifeclass – OWN." <https://www.youtube.com/watch?v=2G7Ds4NgSng>.

compromising the things you may miss from being buried in the sand.

It's critical to pause from time to time to look beyond the goal. Pause and reflect on who is influencing you in this chapter. Is it good, is it healthy, or are you just in motion?

You may learn how to take things as they come in life, but without a conscious plan or clarity, you may find it difficult to measure, determine, or understand your direction for yourself. It can feel overwhelming when you reach a certain level. God gives us guidance towards our goals along the way, but it is important to pause and listen long enough to see and read the signs. This can't always come in a weekend getaway or an afternoon alone.   Those smaller pauses are more effective once you first ask yourself whether you are on the right path or not.

The Power of a Conscious Pause

A conscious pause is the clear definite decision to slow everything in your life that you *can* control. It is not a one-week vacation. It isn't a weekend spent reading a book you love. It is a true hiatus in which you dedicate time to yourself. It is a time to nurture your mind, body, and spirit. Think of it as a sabbatical. It is a time to reflect and actively begin the filtering process.

"Just as a car requires a tune up and an oil change after going a certain distance, so do we. It's part of our healthy maintenance."

Whether you are an adolescent striving to make good grades or an adult working long hours to make ends meet, you can benefit from a pause. A pause does not have a name, face, age, or lifestyle. You don't have to be in a bad place in life to embrace a pause. A pause should be a natural part of your growth cycle. You may experience a conscious pause during major shifts in your journey.

This is such a celebration because it allows us to reconnect with who we are and who we are becoming. Whether we realize it or not, we are growing every day. A new day brings new lessons, experiences, and decisions that change who we are.

All ages and walks of life come with social and cultural expectations: be married by this age, have kids by this age, get this type of job, wear this type of clothing, and believe what your entire family believes.

"A pause is a bold and conscious decision to slow down the external actions that we can control to go inward and upward. This is where we find beautiful discovery about ourselves that we may

have been seeking in the wrong places for an extended period of time."

Take my journey, for example: I have taken pauses my entire life, without even realizing what I was doing. I have always loved to think and daydream. I loved writing, exploring, and learning new things. These were the steps I took to allow myself the freedom to discover who I was.

After a very emotional teenage chapter, I found myself having occasional quiet moments in college. I reached a point where I wanted to get away, start fresh, find myself, and live a stress-free life. Of course, college brought on an entirely new set of challenges, but through those challenges I began to learn the difference between healthy and unhealthy relationships (as much as a girl in her 20's could), goals and dreams, habits and conscious decisions.

The experiences I had in college led up to the moment I decided what my life would be like as an adult. I did everything I could to make sure the direction was crystal clear. I began to say *no* to things that did not make sense, instead of trying to go along with the crowd. I began to protect my voice and my magic, whether it made sense to others or not. Looking back, I am so happy I made that choice early on. I realized then the power of getting clear and following my inner voice. I also see how over-planning can lead to tunnel vision, causing you to begin relying on yourself versus where you are led. We'll save that for a later book.

Every one of us has our own unique gift. We must love ourselves as best we can in the moment. During that chapter of my life, I learned to let go, to move forward, to decline opportunities that were not in alignment with my best self, drop false friendships, and embrace the flow of life.

Everything is seasonal. We will never see the flowers bloom in spring if we choose to stay stuck in winter. We will never enjoy the breeze and beautiful colors of fall if we are afraid of the change that will also come in that season. We are human and this doesn't suggest that we won't grieve or have moments of sadness. I have had many. It's life. Things are constantly changing. The powerful thing is that I have learned that it's okay and it's natural. By allowing ourselves seasons to nurture our own spirit and soul in those quiet moments, we receive the clarity and strength to grow into that stem that will sprout and blossom in its next season. We all need a bold conscious period of time to slow down and pay attention, embrace the present, reflect on the past, and *design our destiny*.

Pause #2

Think about what your life looked like two years ago. Was it better then or now?

Now think back five years. How did your life look? How did it feel? Have your dreams or goals changed?

Create a pie chart of your current schedule and lifestyle. You may choose to jot it down on a scrap piece of paper or get really creative. Whichever you choose, this will give you a visual of where the majority of your time is going. From this exercise, you can determine what aspects of your schedule can be altered to create more time for your conscious pause. Keep it handy and refer back to it as often as needed.

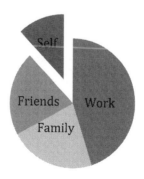

Sometimes we think that because we make a turn onto a road, we are supposed to stay there forever. Then once we reach the end and it's time to take another turn, we experience a great deal of emotion. These are the crossroads- the moments when we have reached a point where we must make a decision.

-Tierra Destiny

TWO

Take Your Power Back: Put Yourself First

Sometimes we spend so much time rationalizing what the *responsible* thing to do is, that we let the thought of spending money on a vacation deprive us of the value those memories could add to our hearts and our family. My mother and grandfather always say *too much of anything isn't good*. That means even too much of the so-called *right* things in life can still leave you out of balance.

Life is meant to be enjoyed. So why do we punish ourselves so much? Imagine how beautiful it would be if we just paused to enjoy the mere fact that we are still breathing. We still have a chance to make a call we've been too afraid to make or send an invitation to connect with someone we admire. We still have the chance to learn something new or let something go. We still have the gift of life.

Pause #3

How we think and *what* we think are the ultimate indicators of how we experience life. Spend some time thinking about how your thought process controls your experiences. Then answer the following questions:

To what extent have I controlled the direction my life has taken?

Do I make decisions for myself, or have I allowed others to make them for me?

How differently would I live my life if I knew that I could not make any mistakes?

What have I accomplished in my last few chapters that makes me feel good? What is it that I keep putting off?

What is it that people always come to me for advice about (This could be a reflection of your gift shining onto the world)?

I know that life can get overwhelming at times. You may say, "Tierra, all of this sounds good, but you don't know me. You have no clue what I am dealing with. You have no clue what I have been through." The truth is, I could say the same thing to you. Don't let a beautiful picture and bright smile make you think that anyone's life is a bed of roses without any thorns.

I have somehow learned to process the storms of life as a time to cleanse the soul, let go and let God, and sit still to welcome the next directional sign in my life; while some people may suffer with feelings and thoughts of constant defeat. If negative thoughts are ruling your life every time a storm comes, please remind yourself that while society views these as bad times, they are the times that give us the wisdom to thrive later. Embrace your process. Don't be ashamed of it. It is all working for your good. Preparing you for greater.

"As long as we are resisting and judging, we will be far away from peace."

- Amandeep Kaur

I recall getting the news about my layoff. I had been home about a week with my second child, and was relaxing in her nursery watching the news. The rumors that my manager assured us were false, were now a reality. Our company was downsizing and I would return to work for thirty days, and then that chapter of my life would end.

What may have felt like devastating news to most, ended up being a blessing for me. So many people were in a panic because they had invested decades into the company. It had literally been their foundation. It was a horrible feeling. I could see the fear in their eyes. What would we do now? What next? We were all forced into the unknown in the blink of an eye. Was it scary? Yes. Was it the end of the world? No. This is a perfect example of the crossroads, a moment in time when you are forced to make a decision. I remember taking time to journal, to research, to ask myself what I really wanted in life and what felt right within. What were my true interests? What had I learned over the years that I could now apply to my next chapter?

I get a visual in my mind when life happens that says *Pause*. This is not the time to press the gas and crash into a ditch. It's your time to slowly let up and pay attention to the inner signals telling you that you are approaching a cliff, or your time on this particular road is ending. That's all.

"Anyone who is still breathing can decide to be the change. Heal. Teach. Inspire. Embrace your purpose and live it until you take your last breath."

After spending time in this exploratory phase, I ran a few of my ideas by those closest to me. I meditated. I prayed. I decided it was time to open my first brick and mortar. Was it scary? Yes. Was it worth every moment? Yes, hands down! I wouldn't trade that chapter for anything in the world. That was one of my biggest leaps of faith and I had no clue how prepared I was and just how important having a corporate background would become.

Sometimes in life we need a challenge to show us what we are made of. I believe we can grow frustrated at times when we are only using a fraction of our gifts. Entrepreneurship will stretch you beyond your wildest dreams. If you aren't careful, you may fall into other pitfalls, or fall into the trap of entrepreneur poverty. It's a mindset that will make you believe *once an entrepreneur, only an entrepreneur.* That was me. I can see a bigger picture now. You can work for yourself and others. Just follow your truth and do what feels best in your current chapter. You are only defined by what you believe.

It was not always this clear for me. Growing up and trying to figure things out can be stressful. I remember working so much overtime after my high school graduation that I fell asleep while driving, less than three minutes from home. Were there signs that I was burnt out in the months prior? Yes. Did I pay attention? No. There will be future chapters in my life where even I will need to pick this book back up. Life is cyclical. We are all stronger in different areas at various times. You may be surprised to know that even during the final editing phase, this very book ministered to my soul and helped me regain my own strength and clarity for the next level of my purpose and journey. Growth is constant. Embrace several fresh starts. Celebrate them. It means you are brave and always striving to improve. Wisdom is our friend.

Many of us (including me) can overthink. I want you to be cautious of this during your pause. Please understand that there is such a thing as analysis paralysis— the state of overthinking a situation to the point that no action is ever taken. This is normally due to an overwhelming fear of success and making the wrong choice.

What if you knew that either decision would still ultimately lead to where you were meant to be? Maybe one is the road less traveled while the other is the traditional route, but you would still end up exactly where you were meant to be. Would that make your decision a little easier? Would you sit still forever and do nothing or spend years trying to do everything just right? Or would you make the choice that is best for you today and not wonder what the next thirty years would hold? We must all know ourselves. We must begin to trust ourselves. Trust that voice inside of you that is leading you to make the right choice.

"The beautiful thing about living your truth is that there is no right or wrong. It's your truth. How you express it is where the choice comes in to play. Internal freedom is a gift we must choose to unwrap."

It's a faith walk, but our choices determine our direction. Even when you take a detour or hit a pothole, never give up. Why would you give up on yourself, your dreams, and your goals? Never allow outside circumstances, people who aren't more special than you, or negative thoughts to stop you from moving forward. Always move inward and upward in a forward direction. Be bold enough to be still until you are strong enough and clear enough to take the next step.

Life can throw us some major blows and it may feel like we are going through ultimate storms with tornado warnings. There are times we can feel like we have absolutely no control of anything. The truth is, the only thing we ever really have control over is ourselves; what we contribute to the world; and how we respond to the everyday unfolding of events, conversations, situations, and our thoughts.

So many of us work really hard trying to do the right thing and reaching for our goals, that we feel completely sideswiped when life happens and we are left to face a new reality. The new reality is what pushes us to explore a new set of emotions as well as a new level of how we want to instinctively react. My girlfriends and I often find ourselves saying, "Whew! I can tell I have grown because if this happened ten years ago, I would have..."

I think we can all attest to the fact that every experience over time helps us reach a higher level of maturity, wisdom, and self-control. The desire to control our reactions, respond in a way that we can be proud of, and in a way that reminds us that we do have control of our mind and decisions, is empowering. I believe this is the inner fulfillment most of us really want: the power to control our own lives when so many other people and experiences have tried to force us to be things we don't want to be and do things we don't want to do.[4] We rarely realize in the heat of the moment that our response can actually change the complete course of events. How is that for control? It all truly starts in the mind. That is why it is so important to protect your mind. Feed your mind.

---

[4] Sifferlin, Alexandra. "How People-Pleasing May Lead to Overeating." *Time*. Time. Web. <http://healthland.time.com/2012/02/02/how-people-pleasing-leads-to-overeating/>.

Take time to pause, examine, and measure where you are mentally, emotionally, and spiritually. Being *aware* allows you to take control of how you are operating in this world. Your life is your world. Decide how you want it to feel and who you want to become.

THREE

Dig In: There's Work During the Pause

Over the years, I have heard so many people say it is important to do the work. *Do your work* is not only a broad statement, but it is also a broad task that will require you to focus and *put yourself first*. Doing your inner work means taking a self-assessment with acceptance.

It is easy for us to observe the behavior of others and the results of their decisions, but we may have difficulty identifying our own habits. This leads to justifying our circumstances and possibly shifting accountability for our actions to others or life events that we have no control over. Of course, there will be unexpected situations in life; however, these situations do not excuse poor reactions or behaviors as a result.

Even after we've identified the areas in our life that need work, on average, it takes over sixty days to form new healthy habits. [5] Doing our inner work causes us to address our habitual actions and face the pain that we have been allowing to linger in our life head on, focusing on the end result of our task rather than the amount of time it will take to complete it.

Pause #4

It takes true courage and vulnerability to look at ourselves and ask the tough questions. Take a moment to reflect and answer the following:

What have I contributed to the conflict or recurring cycle in my life?

How can I improve?

What can I do differently?

To whom do I owe an apology?

---

[5] Lally, Phillippa, Cornelia H. M. Van Jaarsveld, Henry W. W. Potts, and Jane Wardle. "How Are Habits Formed: Modelling Habit Formation In The Real World." *European Journal of Social Psychology* 40.6 (2010): 998-1009. Print.

Who has hurt me? Have I talked about or addressed the pain? Have I truly released it or simply tried to suppress it?

"What's the secret? Answer: Get fed up and get fearless about what you know you deserve! Make a bold decision and create your own standard."

Use Your Pain: Transform It

Pain can be used to propel you to your highest potential or sink you to your lowest downfall. Pain that sits in the soul over time is like a disease that invisibly spreads throughout your body. It takes over your heart and mind, and becomes apparent through your words and actions. Some of us withdraw and push people away; others cling to and thrive off of people to fill the void. When we deal with the pain head on, our relationships become balanced. We are more positive and pleasant to be around.

If pain is still weighing inside of you or rearing its ugly head from time to time, don't ignore it or beat yourself up about it. Face it. Accept it. It's okay for you to feel the things you are feeling. Be brave enough to ask yourself whether you're in a little too deep, off balance, or not involved enough. I encourage you to face those deepest thoughts head on and ask yourself:

Pause #5

Why does this hurt so badly?

What do I wish was different?

How am I better, stronger, or wiser because it happened this way?

What lesson have I learned from the pain that I can now apply to my future?

Transform Your Pain with Gratitude

Sit in that thought for a moment reflecting on how this event may have contributed to your strengths, your wisdom, and your path in life. Find gratitude in it. Can your story help someone else? Being open, accepting that it happened, and sharing it will shift your pain from a toxin to what will fuel you into a new level of your ultimate purpose. Face it, dive in, and release.

I know this is easier said than done. We are human. It's a process. I have struggled with processing pain and rejection as well. I'm constantly trying to fix things that are broken and am often left feeling tired and drained. I now realize that some things simply cannot be fixed. Of course, there are some things that can be, but surrendering to the process allows you to save time and energy that could be used to focus within. With the right spirit and mindset, we become centered and everything eventually falls into place. Everything is working for our good.

"When we let go and flow, we blossom and release our natural fragrance and energy into the world without pressure, stress, or force."

Release

The decision to release negative thoughts, feelings, and behaviors is one of the most empowering things we can do for ourselves. To be honest, I think that most of us try to release things, believe that we have, and become disappointed or defeated when we find ourselves in a similar cycle of emotions yet again.

You may be trying to release the thought or memory of the past instead of doing the inner work we just discussed. Releasing requires facing the entire situation head on, accepting that it happened, finding purpose or gratitude in your ability to overcome, and making a decision to release it in its entirety. You have the right to do so. Accepting that pain has occurred does not define who you are. You are beautiful and amazing. You are an inspiration.

You are probably yearning for inner peace or the power to control your thoughts and emotions. The best way to gain control is to release it and know that you can be whomever you want. You can be positive. You can be happy. You can be loving. You can be all these amazing things if you decide. You are not your past. You are already amazing!

Remember that some of the baggage you are carrying is not your own. You owe it to yourself to pause and do the work required to release your own baggage along with everyone else's. This is something that is very hard for me at times because I'm someone who is constantly making an effort to be conscious and present.

It can be frustrating when memories seem to weigh us down. I have found that reminding myself that I am human and that the hurt served a bigger purpose, keeps me from staying stuck in the past.

When you prepare for a trip, you probably tell yourself to pack light so that you can leave room to bring back something new. It should be the same way for your life. You are not meant to keep everything that you gather along the way. Some things were simply for that season or chapter in your life. You wouldn't pack your winter coat for your summer vacation in the Caribbean. It is important to begin including pauses in your regular life cycle so that you can make conscious decisions about what you are carrying and what you need to let go of.

"Acceptance of our true feelings is one of the most liberating and challenging things to do. We must be patient with ourselves and learn to honor our process in our own time. "

Pause #6

Who are you?

If you could hit reset today, what would be the new vision for your life, your business, and your family?

Are you doing what you believe in?

The desires and vision you have just felt are a great start to manifesting and building your reality. Don't allow the past to dictate what you can build. Never be afraid to start over. You are wiser now. Celebrate that!

The release you've been waiting for is also waiting for you. Make a conscious choice to clear your schedule and become your own project.

-Tierra Destiny

FOUR

Did You Grab the Wrong Bag?

We've heard time and time again that we should let the past be the past. After working extremely hard to come to a point of acceptance with my own past, I learned that very few of us truly understand our past and often have a difficult time embracing all aspects of it.

For me it was like taking all the baggage I had accumulated over my life's journey, sitting it all down on the floor, and literally going through it piece by piece. After doing this, I realized that not all the baggage I carried was mine. There were remnants of stressors and voids from my childhood. There were unhealthy relationships, instances of false love, and wounds from the absence of my father.

We are all carrying things that have nothing to do with us. Most of it has been dumped on us by others we love who more than likely had the same thing done to them. The interactions we have growing up plant seeds in our spirit. Those seeds are tucked in our minds and our hearts, and can resurface when we least expect them. As we go through life striving for the best, we are like human sponges taking all of those life experiences in.

So many of us find ourselves holding on to past experiences and applying them to future situations. I even stop myself now and ask, *Is this fear causing me to proceed with caution or wisdom reminding me not to repeat the past?*

It took me becoming an adult who was willing to look at life from the lens of gratitude, service, and accountability for my choices and contributions before I realized that some of the baggage I was still holding on to only had power because I wasn't willing to let go.

I had to be honest and identify the areas of my life in which I was standing in my own way. I had somehow told myself that if my biological father had always been there that life would have been different. I now realize that what we fantasize about in our mind is not always reality.

There are people who have fathers physically in their lives, but are absent emotionally. Some were abusive. Some were irresponsible and caused financial stress and agony. Why in the world did I live my life assuming life would have been better? The more I get to know my father and accept him for the human being he is, the more I trust the process that all things work as they should.

We are all doing the best we can with what we have. Fantasy is not reality. We harm ourselves when we hold on to what does not exist. The mind is powerful. Once we begin to open ourselves up to think differently and focus on gratitude, we will see how everything has prepared us for this moment. We can learn to slowly accept reality and begin doing our own work within.

While taking the time to sort all those bags that aren't ours, we will run into a few that are. I was very giving, yet self-centered. I wanted things to go my way so that I could predict the outcome and remain in my own world. We simply don't grow that way. Life is not only about what we want and how we think it should be; but learning to listen and process a new way of thinking is not always easy.

Without taking the time to consciously release things that have caused us pain or disappointment, we hinder our growth and development. This can also affect us physically. Feelings of anger and resentment create stress, which can cause increased blood pressure and heart rate. When we hold onto anger and past trauma, the stress response never goes away. [6]

But our journey is what brings wisdom. We must embrace it. There comes a time in our journey that we must accept responsibility for our choices and the outcome of those choices. Instead of focusing on what was done to us, we must focus on taking our power back and put both hands on the steering wheel. Now throw your shades on and ride, while remaining open to the endless possibilities of the journey.

"Sometimes letting go is the best thing to do. When you stop growing, there is usually something else waiting for you. Trying to carry everything along for your entire journey can leave you weighed down, cluttered, and less productive. Make room by letting go and your wings will thank you for giving them room to spread and soar!"

Vulnerability

Never before had I felt safe or courageous enough to admit when I felt vulnerable. Thanks to an episode of *Super Soul Sunday* with Dr. Brené Brown, I learned that being vulnerable allows us to remain open. It doesn't make you weak or mean that you must share your life

---

[6] Goldring, Clarann. "Forgiveness." *Common Sense Psychology Website*. Web. <http://www.commonsensepsychology.com/forgiveness.php>.

story with the world; it means that you are bold and courageous enough to stare fear in the face and say, "I am not going to let this feeling stop me from pushing forward and embracing what could potentially be a beautiful lesson or life experience." In fact, this lesson was so important that I began actively having the most vulnerable conversation to confront my past than I ever had before.

Pause #7

Sometimes our memories cause us to shrink back. Think about your past. Be honest with yourself as you answer the following questions:

Think about your most special childhood memory. What makes it so great?

Years ago, you had a moment that upset you. Does it matter now?

Are you holding on to something you need to let go of?

If you could dump all of your memories into one bag and start over with the wisdom you have learned, what could you accomplish today?

As children we may have experienced things that would be interpreted completely different as adults. Some of us have painful memories that we have swept under the rug. Others may naturally have a gift to process the past for what it is and move forward. Whatever the case, pausing to reflect and conduct a mental and emotional self-evaluation is important. Journaling can be transformative. Counseling allows us to speak openly and freely to someone without judgment. Surrounding yourself with positive people or others who can relate to your story can also be a great tool to consider if you are someone who still has work to do in this area.

Pause #8

Take the next ten minutes to reflect on memories that may be surfacing as you go through this chapter. You may choose to write them down or simply be present in the moment. You may find that you need more time to reflect. Give yourself this time.

"Instead of focusing on the darkness of the past, I now Celebrate the Light from the Stars that never left me and guided me towards my Destiny! I wish the same for you."

Skills and lessons learned in adulthood often have the ability to bring childhood experiences full circle. We are better equipped to understand and deal with the pain and disappointment that we may have found difficult to comprehend as children.

How can anyone reach their full potential without understanding who they are, where they have been, and where they want to go? Life is like the ocean when the tide comes in, rolling from one phase to the next. Understanding who we are internally ensures that the waves never pull us under. A sense of self is priceless. Never let someone take this from you.

Our past may sometimes be painful, but there is so much more to celebrate and to be grateful for. It's hard to do deep inner work while juggling a million other things. We tell ourselves that we are doing well when we take a day out to read or pay a visit to the salon. Doing this consistently is great, but also know when it may be time for a little more. The release you've been waiting for is also waiting for you. Make a conscious choice to clear your schedule and become your own project so that you can examine what you've outgrown, acknowledge those things that have not been settled from your past, let them go, and move forward.

Pause #9

A *conscious pause* not only allows you to reflect on your past, but it also allows you to celebrate the healing that occurs on your journey. It is a time to soak in gratitude and really admire *you*. How often do we stop to just love on ourselves? Let's take a moment to do that:

Make a list of everything that you love about yourself.

What makes me special, unique and beautiful?

How is the world better because of me?

What have I overcome?

What struggles did I face that only made me stronger?

What have I accomplished that I no longer give myself credit for?

How have I uplifted another person, educated another person with my life experiences, or taken the time to simply help someone out?

♦ ♦ ♦

"Our deepest fear is not that we are inadequate. Our deepest fear is that we are powerful beyond measure. It is our light, not our darkness that most frightens us. We ask ourselves, 'Who am I to be brilliant, gorgeous, talented, fabulous?' Actually, who are you not to be? You are a child of God. Your playing small does not serve the world. There is nothing enlightened about shrinking so that other people won't feel insecure around you. We are all meant to shine, as children do. We were born to make manifest the glory of God that is within us. It's not just in some of us; it's in everyone. And as we let our own light shine, we unconsciously give other people permission to do the same. As we are liberated from our own fear, our presence automatically liberates others."[7]

Marianne Williamson

---

[7] Williamson, Marianne. *A Return to Love: Reflections on the Principles of a Course in Miracles.* New York, NY: Harper Collins, 1992. Print.

PART II

It's Possible:
Real Women Share Their Pauses

"Stripped away of the titles and the mask that I had worn for so many years, suddenly I was just *me*. I gave myself permission to honestly assess where I was in life, what was working well, and what needed to be adjusted."

-Eardie M. Houston

FRESH START

"I needed my own personal circle of the best business and spiritual advisors to help me on my journey. I found those people and I am so grateful. Now I can see myself opening up and being brave. I start my day fueling my mind and spirit. I watch what I eat. I keep negativity out. I listen to wise counsel and now I see my business picking up again. Seeds that I had sown years ago can now be harvested."

THOUGHTS FROM THE HEART
of
Ursula Harrington

FIVE
THE MASK OF SUCCESS
by Eardie M. Houston

On the surface, everything seemed perfect. After a difficult past, I had overcome abuse, abandonment, and poverty; and achieved personal and professional *success*. Over time, however, I became increasingly aware that I wasn't living my life purposefully. The salary, company car, and frequent flier miles no longer seemed like enough. I realized that while I had been chasing money, status, and all of the trappings of so-called *success,* I was certain that I hadn't even begun to scratch the surface of my true purpose and what I was truly supposed to do with my time, energy, and resources.

"Despite the awareness of the nudge in my heart, I pushed against it and kept going along the path that was most familiar."

It felt safe. But after a while, it became uncomfortable. Mildly uncomfortable at first, but the discomfort progressed until it was just plain painful. There was no doubt that I was out of alignment with my purpose. I was not quite clear about what my purpose was, but I was certain that the outward appearance of success wasn't it. So with the support of my husband, I made the decision to press the pause button for a while. To the shock of many in my life, I walked away from a successful career in order to deliberately be still.

The first thing I had to learn to do was rest. I know. Sounds like that should be something instinctive, but for me, it took effort. I had no idea of how tightly wound I was! For the first month or so, I would wake up in panic in the middle of the night, worrying about deadlines and quotas, as I so often did before the pause. It was as if I had a form of PTSD. My body and mind had to be conditioned to relax. I had to make a deliberate effort to learn to rest.

I relinquished control, or rather finally began to embrace the fact that so much of life is outside of my control. Of course, there were some things that were my part, but I lived in a constant state of heightened stress because of my desire to control everything. There's such a peace that comes with learning how to surrender. I've learned that over these past few months. And I'm thankful for that lesson.

My pause has been such a transformative experience. I had no idea how engrossed I had become in external things that had no real worth.

During my pause, I've been blessed with the opportunity to reconnect with my true core, and not the image of who I thought I should be. I meditate. I journal. I enjoy stillness. I've gotten real with myself, which has allowed me the vulnerability to be real with others. I was surprised by how much energy I had been expending in an effort to force myself to stay in places that were never supposed to be permanent. Sure, many of my experiences have been enriching and I've learned a lot along the way, but I've realized that life isn't supposed to be static. I'm supposed to grow, change, and embrace different seasons of my life. I realized my tendency to fear risks and *play it safe*. I also now realize that the biggest risk of all is really the risk of not becoming who I am supposed to be.

As a result of this period and the lessons that I've learned, I now have a clearer direction. After shutting off the noise in life for a while, not only do I know my purpose, but I am also on the path towards living my purpose. I now feel reinvigorated and alive. There's great value in stopping to ask yourself, *Why am I doing this? Out of habit? Or out of purpose?* I've come to realize that a lot of the habits that I've developed over the years were necessary to get me out of the difficulty of my past. However, that was long ago, and many of those habits don't serve me well anymore. So I've given myself permission to change courses. To tell myself a different story.

For anyone that is currently in the place that I was prior to my pause, I would encourage them to pay attention to that tug in their spirit. Instinctively, we know when we're out of alignment. Oftentimes, our reaction may be to ignore it, to press onward, to keep *doing what we've got to do*. However, I would challenge you to consider taking a moment to turn off the noise. It may not be months, or weeks. Perhaps a weekend, or start with a day. Just stop for a moment. Consider the possibility that things could be different. Better. It's not selfish to nurture yourself. And sometimes, a pause may be exactly what you need.

SAY *NO*

"I learned the art of listening to myself and that it's okay to say *no* sometimes....I learned that pausing is not a sign of weakness, but a sign of *strength and wisdom*!"

THOUGHTS FROM THE HEART
of
Cynthia D. King

SIX

Infidelity: The Power of Forgiveness
by **Connie Phillips-Gilbert**

In July 2007, my mind felt numb from the shock of my reality. I was so very angry. How dare he? How dare he betray me like this? My marriage was scarred. The embarrassment. Oh my God. How did this happen to me? As I hurried, as fast as I could to get my three-year-old baby out of the house, I packed one suitcase filled with winter clothes on one of the hottest days of the year. My husband stood near the car, repeatedly asking me not to leave. How dare he?

In a matter of one week, a marriage counseling session, and one night without my husband, it was evident that he had cheated on me. How did this happen? We knew each other so well. Sure enough, we had experienced a hard blow in our finances, but we had a plan. I was to devote my time to caring for our three-year-old son, as we had agreed this was the best option for at least one year. He was supposed to be out working to support us, to regain our stability.

I couldn't breathe. I had to get out of Atlanta. I had to get away from my crazy husband. I didn't know him anymore. He didn't even look like my husband. I drove straight to my mom's house in my hometown, Soperton, Georgia. For the next several months, I devoted my time to self-preservation. I needed to survive, and I did so by taking care of my son's day-to-day needs. I walked, cried, and prayed alone every time I felt sad or angry, which was frequent. My emotions were out of control.

I decided to attend our local church every Sunday. I wrote in my journal often. I also screamed into the pages often. My Bishop had requested that I call her every two weeks to let her know how I was doing, and I did.

I picked up and read the Bible to better understand how God would punish my husband for what he did to me. My mind and heart were so full. I observed other families in this small community, realizing that even though things were not perfect and they probably fought, they were still together as a family. What happened to us?

Although, my family was supportive, I knew that I could not stay there forever. As much as I wanted to hide and be angry, I knew I had to return and face my demons. In February 2008, I returned to Atlanta, not knowing what awaited me upon my arrival. But I knew I could no longer keep my son away from his father. I concluded that no matter how I felt towards *him*, it was not fair to punish my son. So, in my little Toyota Tercel, I packed all of our belongings and headed to my cousin's house. I was invited to stay there while I figured out my next steps. I knew it was imperative to set ground rules between my husband and myself upon my return to the city. I declared that we were like two banks with one vested interest--our son.

Although my husband had failed me terribly, I would not allow him to disrupt my son. So, once a week, we met at Borders so that my son could have time with his father. I enrolled my son into a small private Christian-based school so that I could find a job and get back on track. Because we had a son together, I had to communicate with my husband on a regular basis. How horrible was that? Could I have been punished any worse? I did not want to deal with him.

Now here back in the city, I had to figure out a routine that worked for my son and me. I immediately reconnected with my church. Now, every Sunday, we had something to do and somewhere to go. Routinely my husband called every night to say goodnight to our son, and we met every week at Borders. Still, we argued with each other about our failed marriage. I could not see any hope for us as a couple. How could I ever trust him again? How could I forgive him for the betrayal and embarrassment? My heart was still angry.

Then, my church announced a class called *Before You Divorce*. I just knew this class was going to provide me the answers I needed for how to divorce this man. I didn't want him and he did not deserve to have someone like me.

There were five sessions. The class facilitator was the same person who directed our wedding a few years before. My first thought was *How did I arrive here?* Then, all the emotions started to surface again: sadness, anger, hopelessness, and self-pity. At the beginning of each session, the facilitator kept a box of Kleenex in arm's reach. I had the full intention to be an active participant in class, learn, and share. On the contrary, I, like many others in the class, cried through at least two full sessions. No one judged. It just happened.

At the closing of this class, I understood that if I was going to survive this mind-numbing, heart-wrenching pause in my life, it would require me to invest the time and work necessary to regain my footing spiritually, physically and financially. I had to stop focusing on revenge. I had to stop blaming my husband for everything. I had to *forgive*. But how could I forgive and forget this horrible thing that he did to me/our family? I had to understand that the act of *forgiving* was the pathway to my healing. It would be my freedom and release from the mental prison that I created in my own mind.

So, without emotions and real commitment to the idea, I decided to practice forgiving by just thinking about it. Before long, I was verbalizing it out loud. Although, we still had disagreements, I could hear and receive my husband saying that he was sorry for what happened. With such feedback from him, I was no longer angry or felt I needed to make him suffer for what he did. My focus was different. This allowed me to take control of my hopes and dreams.

Months later, I stumbled upon Iyanla Vanzant's book, *Living Through the Meantime*. The first chapter suggested that the "very ground where I stood, on that day, that moment in time," was indeed, "Holy Ground." Oh my God. She knew how I felt during my difficult journey. This was a sign or confirmation. I knew instantly that I would survive. I knew that God, Himself, was with me. I began my quest to redefine me. I had to ask myself the hard questions and be prepared for the truth. With or without my husband, I was important enough to fight for me.

In late 2009, we recovered. I don't remember exactly when the transition occurred, but somehow we were back under one roof. Our marriage weathered the storm. There was still much healing to be done. New trust had to be built. My husband and I became active participants in the efforts to strengthen our marriage. With the help of God, we found the way back to each other. We stood and fought everything and everyone that tried to destroy us. We knew that we had a testimony. There was no taking our marriage lightly. We would win together.

LOVE YOURSELF

"I learned that panic is just an overreaction to life's circumstances.... So, in order to overcome my overreaction, I had to learn to rest in the unconditional love that God already had for me.... That unconditional love now influences me to see and respond to life by way of love. I live life out loud now and I am loving it!"

THOUGHTS FROM THE HEART
of
Rhonda Glaze

SEVEN

Inner Peace
by **Felicia Joy**

I have been in *pause* mode for the past two years. Initially, it was not conscious. I was burnt out and falling apart unbeknownst to other people. I felt totally depleted in every way. I prayed, asking God for help. The answer came as an intense desire to go to a ten-day total silence meditation retreat that I had read about long before that moment.

I went to the retreat and experienced an incredible spiritual breakthrough. After that, my pause became a conscious decision. I took a sabbatical to really explore the things that had come to my conscious awareness during my meditation retreat.

My pause was triggered by a feeling of depletion. I had done, and was doing, all the things that our general culture prescribes as pillars of happiness. I still found myself unhappy. I felt that certain people and circumstances in my life were making me unhappy. Yet, I also could see a pattern where I was inviting those people and circumstances into my life. I wanted to understand what was happening so I could eliminate the pattern once and for all.

The lessons and revelations I had during my sabbatical—or *pause*—are numerous. In fact, I had so many of them that I wrote a book entitled *Why Are You Settling for Less?* to discuss and share them with other people.

Essentially, what I discovered is that there is the *Accumulated Self* and the *Aspirational Self*. Many times the reason we cannot take hold of, or keep hold of, the life of peace and plenty that we desire is because we are attempting to forge ahead toward a vision from the Aspirational Self, yet we still are living and behaving as the Accumulated Self. This automatically, every time, without question, without fail—regardless of who the individual is—will cause friction, stress, strain, and crisis, especially if the individual is not aware of what is happening.

One other lesson and revelation among many others I have found: every person has a *P Spot*—a Purpose Spot. They can either choose their purpose, follow an inspired purpose, or fall into purpose. When we hear the word *purpose*, we automatically think of a positive, productive and powerful agenda. Not necessarily so. Literally, a purpose is something that draws you in and drives you each day. Some people have long-term purpose. Some people's purpose shifts daily or weekly.

Depending on a person's accumulations, if they are not living in awareness and not choosing or accepting an inspired purpose, then they can easily fall into negative purpose. This is what has driven the celebrity crazed and blog gossip culture we now have. Some people have unwittingly established the purpose of being nosy and critical of others. Of course, this also goes beyond celebrities. It happens in families, schools, and offices every day.

People who are not aware of their personal issues, and who have not consciously chosen or accepted a positive purpose, must still live in purpose because that's the way we are built. But their purpose, unfortunately, is a wayward one. People can turn from this once they realize they are in it.

A simple, straightforward way to think of this is to ask yourself, "What did I spend my time doing today that positively moved my life, or the life of others, forward?" I dare say that a whole lot of people would be embarrassed at their answer on most days. That's how you determine whether you are living with purpose that matters.

What made my *pause* so powerful for me was that I thought I had my act together. Please. Not even close. I was always a spiritual person, but there were so many layers. I have been rebuilt from the inside out. Hallelujah!

People might be surprised to know that I went through a long stretch of fear. Fear would never be a word that anyone would have associated with me. I have always been known to be fearless and courageous, and I always was. During this sabbatical though, there were rough periods. Now, I have truly learned how to walk on water—faithfully and fearlessly.

I also went through being rudderless and feeling unmotivated. Before, I was so driven by the need to accomplish things that others would admire. After my spiritual breakthrough, and meditating regularly, I experienced such incredible peace that I did not care about any of that. So my hunger and drive were gone. It was a beautiful place to be, spiritually and psychologically, but impractical for daily life as an entrepreneur. I had to work through that very carefully.

I have so much respect and admiration for people who go against the grain and who have worked to change and be better. I have so much love and compassion for people who are trapped within their accumulations and do not even realize it.

"I overcame my accumulations. A need to accomplish to fill a void. A need to be accepted. A need to eat away stress. I overcame anger. I overcame misplaced emotion. I overcame the impulse to be silent and keep the peace when I really wanted to speak. I overcame culture—trying to be a particular way to be accepted as a professional, a black girl, an entrepreneur, whatever. I am—that's it. Take it or leave it."

My advice to anyone contemplating a pause is simple: follow your spirit. It will unfailingly guide you. Your inner spirit knows what you need. If you are not spiritual, call it whatever you need to call it to accept it—but everyone has it. Follow it and become weightless, free and experience a joy like no other. Peace.

PAUSE FOR FAMILY

"Never forget the importance of family, friends and faith…. We're sometimes trained to think that people are more hurtful than helpful. I am a non-believer of this philosophy and have witnessed first-hand that God places angels and support systems in our lives to help us through obstacles. Never look at what you think you're losing, look at what you'll gain. I can always get another job. I will never have another mother.

THOUGHTS FROM THE HEART
of
Lisa 'L.A.' Matthews

EIGHT

Almost Married
by Joy McLaughlin

As I sat in my bed one late afternoon, I thought about the conversation I'd had earlier that day with my boyfriend Tramaine. We'd been dating less than ninety days, yet on the other end of the phone, he was asking me to marry him.

This seemed way too good to be true. The first words that came to me were from my mentor Tierra Destiny Reid saying, "Things look different from a distance than they do close up." I knew that I needed a moment to clearly assess what was taking place. I took a deep breath, closed my eyes, and paused.

I didn't accept any calls from him that night. I noticed that he's started posting our pictures on

Facebook and really made it known on social media that I was the only thing that existed in his life.

I recalled how much time he spent in the mirror. It was often longer than I did. When I would introduce him to people, he went above and beyond with compliments. Once I thought about it, he was just too much for me. The reality was that I could not marry Tramaine. I looked deeper during this pause to ask myself why I fell for him. I had to admit that I struggled with insecurity. Tramaine came into the picture complimenting me, which really boosted my ego. He told me how amazing I was and I was eating it up!

I had been traveling a lot more while dating Tramaine. He was funding all of our trips and I was happy because he was making it happen. But was I really happy?

My pillow was soaked from tears after realizing I was not allowing God to affirm who I was and that I was really basing my happiness on what Tramaine was making happen for me. Along with his physical attributes, the money, trips, shopping, and compliments were what kept me smiling.

Tears flowed constantly at the memory of the text messages that I could no longer ignore. Text messages from another man telling Tramaine how good he looked wearing his underclothes in the picture that was sent to him. Or the one from yet another guy telling Tramaine that he would keep him warm on his return back from a trip we were on together. The rush for marriage with me was a cover up for the fact that he loved both men and women.

Pausing showed me the signs were there the entire time. I was just so close and in love that it took me stepping back and looking at things from a distance. I had the hard conversation and broke it off with Tramaine.

I am still in my healing process today, but I am a much stronger woman as a result of the lessons learned from this relationship. I now allow God to affirm who I am in him. My happiness is based on my confidence in who God has called me to be and knowing that he is my source.

If you find yourself in a relationship where you don't have peace, don't ignore the signs that are clearly displayed. Take a pause and look at what drew you to this person to see if there is an empty void in you that this person may be fulfilling. Look at the patterns of things they do in the relationship. Pausing changed my life and I know it can do the same for you.

REGRET NOTHING

"I regret nothing anymore because every season of my life I have experienced thus far has stretched me, molded me, and pushed me to grow into the woman I am today and the one I am still becoming."

THOUGHTS FROM THE HEART
of
Delmar Johnson

NINE

Behind the Curtain: Fear of Success
by **Kaira Akita**

My conscious pause started with a forced one. In 2010, I made the decision with my then fiancé (now husband), to make the permanent move from Atlanta to Los Angeles. We're both in the entertainment business and after some successful work in Atlanta, we knew it was time to make the move to the city that would truly build our careers.

Little did I know, this move was less about my career and more about my ultimate purpose and discovering my actual self. Gigs were slow (that's putting it politely), so I kept busy with my own creative projects and entrepreneurial passions. I enjoyed them all, but I was unhappy. And although I enjoyed acting - a lot - I've never felt like I was meant to be just an actress. I dabbled in a lot of things, and they all made sense to me. But what didn't make sense was why I felt like I was always on a wheel, but not getting as far as I wanted.

I was sick and tired of pretending to appreciate compliments from strangers, friends, and colleagues who said things like, "You're always doing something, always reinventing yourself!" The truth was, I still didn't know or understand who I really was or what I even wanted. What others saw as excellence was as easy as breathing to me. I knew that there was little effort on my part for the things that were happening in my life and I felt like a fraud. I was mentally and emotionally exhausted and I hadn't even gotten started! This is when I decided I had to do something different and consciously hit *pause*.

It was a slow, painful process because it forced me to take a really hard look at myself without the usual distractions. No big ideas to work on, no social media, no keeping up with so and so, no auditions.

"And when all that went away, the layers of self-doubt, fear, paralysis, and wanting validation from others revealed themselves for what they were. It wasn't just a problem for my career; it had become part of my self-identity and woven into my relationships, choices, and everyday thoughts and interactions. "

I was forced to have uncomfortable conversations with friends, relatives, and yes, myself. I had to go back to the basics and discover who I was, not just busy my days away hiding behind what I could do. As long as I focused on what I could do, I knew I could hide in plain sight. This was because I never felt people would appreciate me beyond my gifts, for just being me. But I realized I was the culprit of my feelings of inadequacy. I felt uncomfortable with defining myself beyond my gifts. They've always defined me, and that's all I knew. I never felt I was a good person, a good daughter, a good sister, a good friend. And so I would overcompensate with my talents, self-sabotage, and allow myself to stay stuck in unhealthy "underdog" syndrome situations. Yes, it truly got that deep once I allowed myself to surrender and let go of the world I had created for myself. I couldn't believe it.

Ultimately, my pause allowed me to gain personal and spiritual focus, strengthen my relationships and inner circle (trust, when you're not in fast forward mode, a lot of people fall by the wayside!), and to make room for my gifts to flow naturally and serve my greater purpose. I now feel confident about who I am with and without my gifts, and I can define success on my own terms. Another unexpected, but much appreciated side effect: it helped me to recognize and draw like-minded people and opportunities. Sort of a "real recognizes real" thing going on. It's pretty freaking amazing.

Today I see my pause as a way of life more than a moment in time. Yes, there's a time to sit still and a time to move, but the perspective of the pause fuels my "play" moments. Plus, as I move from level to level, I know I will experience many more pause moments. It is a necessary part of personal and professional growth. Funny, I was so scared to pause for fear I'd be left behind. But the truth is, my pause has shown me an entirely different level of living, one that's truly worth waiting for.

I'm just entering the season beyond my pause, and while it may look like I'm starting over to the naked eye, I'm actually way ahead of the game. I encourage you to do the same! Press pause now so your extraordinary life can play out later. I promise, you won't regret it.

PROGRESSION

"It is okay to fall back and breathe.... We do not have to be Superwoman. We don't have to do it all. We can pause to get clarity, redirect and renew. All I can say is *pause for progress.*"

THOUGHTS FROM THE HEART
of
Annelle Johnson Elder

TEN

Thank You Mom: Single Parenthood
by **Tierra Destiny Reid**

Growing up with a single mother prepared me for the real world. While statistics say that the percentage of children born to single mothers is increasing, I am grateful for the ultimate decision my mother made to leave an abusive relationship and relocate with two children.[8]

In life, I have met several women who remain in relationships because of their own comfort and personal needs. The children seem to be a second thought; however, my mother took the time to get

---

[8] Huffington, Christina. "Single Motherhood Increases Dramatically For Certain Demographics, Census Bureau Reports." *The Huffington Post.* TheHuffingtonPost.com, 1 May 2013. Web. <http://www.huffingtonpost.com/2013/05/01/single-motherhood-increases-census-report_n_3195455.html>.

support and work multiple jobs at once to make a way. Her ability to pause, pray, and move forward with her decision ultimately changed the trajectory of our future.

Instead of growing up seeing black eyes, knock out fights, drugs, and disease, my mother found the strength to make a bold move into the unknown to protect her children. This would ultimately give me the opportunity to see a better way of life. Now, almost thirty years later, I look back in awe and endless gratitude. To move to an entirely new state with two children and only one thousand dollars is beyond a walk of faith. Courage, strength, and determination to change reality are traits that would later be embedded in me as a woman. While it was a very tough road filled with a wide range of emotions and experiences for all of us, I now understand how difficult it can be to decide to choose the unknown in lieu of the predictable. To choose possible happiness over a living hell. Love over war. Peace over numbed pain.

As children we expect our parents to have all the right answers and make all the right decisions. We hold them to an unrealistic standard, forgetting that they are human beings also. Human beings who have emotions, fears, doubts, hopes, dreams, and a past. A past that could be filled with pain, rejection, insecurity, abandonment, love, joy, hope, ridicule, or any number of things. People can only give what they have. One of my greatest lessons learned has been to extend the love, compassion, and understanding that I hope will be extended to me. I wish this for you as well. Be bold and brave in your decisions and trust that everyone is being who they are and doing the best they can at the time.

Many times we can't see beyond how our decisions impact our immediate situation. Think five years out. How would following your honest truth change life for your children and their wellbeing?

"There are some seasons in life that you will walk with others, but sooner or later there comes a time that we must walk alone."

-Annelle Johnson Elder

When my mom said this to me, I meditated on it. I had an overwhelming feeling of comfort the next morning. With God by our side and in our soul, we are never really alone, but we must be willing to embrace that intimate journey within.

If it had not been for my mother's courage and willpower to let go and step out on faith, I would not be the woman I am today. I would not have the perspective on life that I have. I would not be the woman who is able to write this book and share that lesson with you.

Because of my mother's example as a single mother, I am very passionate about supporting single women who are working hard to create a better future for themselves and their children.

My mother's courage and strength is a constant reminder to me and I hope it becomes a reminder to you. Sometimes letting go is the healthiest step into our next chapter. The power of surrender allows God to move on our behalf.

TAKE TIME FOR YOU

"...I would advise others to embrace their pause moments. As women, most of us face the battle of maintaining balance on almost a daily basis. It's so important to your wellbeing to take time for you in the midst of it all. How can we continually pour into others, but not back into ourselves without ending up on empty.... 'Remember to always refuel your tank so that you are better positioned to help someone who needs a little refueling themselves.'"

THOUGHTS FROM THE HEART
of
S.Press

PART III

You're in the Pause. Now What?

"So I've *paused*. Now what? Do I just do nothing and just *be*? Not hardly. What I soon found out was that there is still activity during the pause; it's just targeted, personal and purposeful…. The power of the pause for me was experiencing it as a sacred place, a moment in time, which will happen again."

-*Lorea M. Sample*

ELEVEN
Getting Clear

Over the past few years, I have had dreams and experienced many of them becoming a reality. It literally sent me over the edge when I realized that I was having lunch and sitting right next to Ms. Oprah Winfrey. She had inspired me for several years through her sense of self, purpose, and helping others and I'd convinced myself that this dream wouldn't happen for years. I told myself I would be old by the time it manifested. Well, I was wrong.

I had experienced a shift in my journey just before being invited to this amazing event. A shift, which began when I visited the Grand Canyon for the first time. During the visit, it seemed as if everything in my being had come to a screeching halt. The first sight of the canyon took my breath away and I felt a bit emotional. It was such a powerful sight to see. It was larger than any manmade creation I had ever laid eyes on. A creation beyond words, indeed.

In that moment God was telling me to be still. I kept having a thought that I had reached a pivotal place in my journey. A thought telling me that I had not caught up with myself. I was operating like the woman I was three years prior and I had not allowed all the wisdom and lessons I'd learned to process fully so that I could embrace who I had become.

I slowly began to shift. The whisper in my heart felt like a roar in my soul. I began to change my schedule, way of life, and began my conscious inner journey. I dove within. I began watching *Oprah's Lifeclass* back to back, asking the tough questions, reading books that would challenge the behavior that I had justified for years, and ultimately understanding who I was becoming. *The Untethered Soul* by Michael Singer stopped me in my tracks when he gave the example that explains how a dog that is restricted by an invisible fence will stop trying to travel beyond the yard after getting struck a few times. If the dog was able to endure the pain and push past the fear, he would find that the entire world is just a jump away.[9]

---

[9] Singer, Michael A. *The Untethered Soul: The Journey Beyond Yourself.* Oakland, CA: New Harbinger Publications, 2007. Print.

That very chapter encouraged me to explore the leaps I had taken and those I hadn't.

As an emerging public figure with a purpose to encourage women and the community, social media became a helpful platform that connected me to the world. But for the first time in a long time, I had to pull back. Instead of my normal routine, I used social media in ways that I knew would propel me to new levels in my journey and give me the tools needed to further motivate the women I wanted to reach. I spent several months on twitter with fellow OWN Ambassadors who were like a breath of fresh air amidst the rush. It truly felt like an escape into a deeper level of thinking, feeling, and acceptance.

I had no idea that Oprah would follow me on twitter. That day, I'd had a really rough morning and couldn't wait for *Lifeclass* to begin. When my phone chimed and it said *Oprah Winfrey followed you*, I literally screamed and fell back against the wall. My heart raced and my kids said, "Mommy, are you okay?" Everyone knows how much I admire Oprah. God used that moment to get my full attention. I was one hundred percent committed and ready to do my work. I had no idea that *Lifeclass* would never end. It was a new way of living.

Long story short, a few months later I was finally in Los Angeles. I met fellow Ambassadors face to face and it felt amazing. DeVon Franklin treated us to a very welcoming breakfast and words of inspiration to set the tone. He opened up our minds and hearts with a message that encouraged us to expect and embrace our harvest. I was halfway through his book, *Produced by Faith,* and had a feeling that I was exactly where I was supposed to be. What's even more amazing is that he referenced Bishop T. D Jakes during our time together. I had just attended *Woman Thou Art Loosed* in Atlanta. There, we declared that it was time to *peck* our way out. What was once your provision has become your prison. *Peck* your way out. Well guess what road we passed on the way to meet DeVon three weeks later in L.A.? *Peck* road. I see you GOD.

The next day I covered the red carpet at Oprah's event in support of Little Pink Book and our joint mission to support and encourage women. I wanted to share all the advice with other women who were unable to leave work or travel to attend. The experience was amazing. I didn't use that opportunity to ask about the brands the speakers were wearing, but instead asked what advice each speaker had for women looking to design their destiny.

I will never forget my very first interview with butterflies in my stomach. Martha Beck. I fell in love with her. I remember asking her what advice she had for entrepreneurs:

"Get Rest! Tired nights and months are one thing, but tired decades are a different animal."
- Martha Beck

Instantly I knew that message was for me. I would not be the same on my flight home.

◆◆◆

Lunch with Oprah was full of happiness, joy, and warmth. I was anxious and excited at the same time. When I walked up to Oprah and she said, "Tierra Destiny, how was Bishop Jakes' Conference in Atlanta?" all I could do was smile.

I eventually responded, "It was great." We embraced and I felt like I was five again.

My very first connection with Oprah had been watching her show as a young girl with my mother. Through those moments, I learned the importance of having vulnerable conversations and not holding those feelings in. I was finally here. Wow! It felt amazing. As I sat there for a moment, I drifted away from the room in my mind and said, *God, I hear you and I will rise up to my responsibility to spread the wisdom, joy, peace, and courage that has been poured into me.*

"When it is meant to be, you don't have to force anything. Let it flow!"

So, I made a bold and conscious decision to pause and enjoy all the things I had worked so hard towards. During this time, I began to trust my ability to attract anything I could possibly envision in my mind. I was blown away by the power of God's timing. Even before the amazing trip to Los Angeles to meet Oprah, I had literally checked off twenty years worth of dreams in three short years.

It was very clear to me that all these things were finally happening because I was willing to do the work. It also occurred to me that many people never reach this point because they never really pause to enjoy the journey. We have to be courageous enough to become our own priority. This is the only way to develop that internal alert that says *you have done a lot and are on track; now pause, reflect, restore, and prepare for your next climb.*

"Enjoy the climb. It is only from the top that you are able to see the next mountain. Once you make it to the peak, sit there for a while. Enjoy the view. You've worked hard to get here."

Too often, as women, we push ourselves to run further, but never allow ourselves a real pause to ensure that:

93

- We are operating on full
- We have truly processed the lessons picked up along the way
- We've pulled back enough to look at the next big picture and whether our goals align with our purpose

"So many times we spend years trying to figure out what we are MEANT to do. What is our purpose? But as time passes, I have realized that understanding what you are NOT MEANT to do is half the battle! If you don't enjoy it, move on!"

Purpose

How many people are seeking to discover what their ultimate purpose is? Millions! There is an entire industry devoted to coaching people into find their passion because no one wants to leave this earth without knowing they absolutely served their purpose while here. Let me save you lots of time and money. **It starts inside of you**.

The truth is that if you just pay attention, you will find that *you're already serving your purpose in some form or fashion*. Maybe you are not giving your current contributions to life the value they deserve. Perhaps you are seeking fulfillment to avoid facing emptiness or a set of fears. On the other hand, maybe you believe that your purpose should also be the occupation that provides financial security.

Purpose vs. Profit

Many people feel lost if they are doing what they love, but no money is coming. Yes, you could turn your passion into a business model, but who says you have to? If you have no desire whatsoever to create a business plan, invest in a building and employees, and make strategies, simply doing and enjoying your passion is enough. There are people with millions of dollars who are passionate about what they do, but there are also many who are unfulfilled.

If we continue to tell ourselves that our passion is not our purpose because it does not attract money, we are aligning ourselves with disappointment. It's okay to have something you love that will not bring you monetary gain.

Money may actually be the reward of following your passion if your purpose in life aligns with financial or business success and you are determined enough to keep learning and growing.

For instance, I love helping people. I am a giver. I am a social butterfly. No one is a stranger to me. I am passionate about connecting with people. Does this guarantee that money will come? I don't know. What I know is that my personal passion to connect with people could or could not attract money and I would still be passionate about people.

Let's flip the coin. I love earning my own money. I am passionate about being independent and self-sufficient. This passion fuels my work ethic. This trait results in business opportunities that do attract money. It's the passion that fuels the work ethic that attracts opportunities.

Embrace the difference you make. Give it more value. Don't try to make something into everything. What do I mean by that? If you love to sew, then sew. If you love to sew for yourself and others for pure enjoyment, that is enough. If you sew and enjoy making extra money, then great. That is enough. But just because you begin making extra money does not mean you should quit your job and sew for a living, and that because you are following your passion, the money will come. This truly misleads people into putting themselves into a box. There are other factors to consider when discovering and developing your passion. A great example is Oscar winning actress Lupita Nyong'o. While her career is acting, she has found her passion in styling hair. She loves to braid, but she does not feel comfortable with accepting money from her friends and family. It's just something she loves to do.

You could spend years studying accounting, business, and marketing; all to realize it's simply a passion that people are willing to pay you for. That in itself does not constitute building a business. Yes, your passion attracted money, but that does not mean your purpose is to build a business.

These are the core values that people skip over when they are wondering if they should turn their passion into a business because they like it and people are paying them:

- Intent
- Goal
- Desire
- Commitment
- Work Ethic
- Resources
- Lifestyle
- Capital

Even if you do decide to explore the possibility of building a business from your passion, your purpose will not leave you. The power of a pause can be the solution needed to avoid a few detours along the way, but God loves us so much that even detours sometimes provide lessons we needed to learn.

How many times do we veer off track and wonder how we got there? This happened to me many times during my years of study at the University of Georgia, where the parties outweighed the study sessions and the date nights outweighed my days getting to know myself. Although I did spend a considerable part of my college years embracing emotional pauses and examining my relationships, a pause from work to examine myself would have been really wise at that time. My years in college were in constant motion. I told myself it was for survival, that I had three jobs while attending school because I had to. Looking back now, I realize it was to maintain my lifestyle.

At the time, I may have only been working hard for the newest clothes or to have spending money on the weekends, but that same work ethic has carried over to what I am doing today. It may have taken me much longer to discover my purpose had I not gone through those experiences in college.

Don't underestimate the ability of your past to provide just the fuel you need to get where you are meant to be. It's important to be able to find your silver lining and tap into your inner strength. Sometimes we may need an extra push to get to the next level of clarity and focus, but the real work begins within. Your purpose is already inside of you.

I have found that as long as you have a desire and a dream to do more and seek the resources to do it, it will happen and things will become available to you. When they do, you must take action.

Pause #10

There is something that you do differently than others. What is it?

What is holding you back from the one thing that you really want to do?

Shift

The true shift comes when you decide to do something *different*. Be *something different*. It can be one of the most rewarding and challenging times of your life. You can be pumped up and motivated one day, and doing everything to keep from going back to the same habits the next. Don't beat yourself up. It's normal. We all go through this, but never give up on your goal. One day you will do it. Keep at it! The pivotal moment happens when the decision is final. Most things do not happen the first time around. The shift begins with a mental decision. Our actions must follow.

Self-Evaluation

Are you a giver? Do you love serving others? While this is a great personality trait to have, anything in excess could still be unhealthy.

This was again a huge eye opener because people around us can take advantage of this and you will find yourself feeling disappointed or drained. I realized that it was my responsibility to get clear, healthy, and do what I wanted simply because I wanted to, not because of other people.

Some people are pleasers who say *yes* without a second thought, even when they want to say *no*. Others say *yes* because they feel obligated to be nice or helpful. I realized that I love helping, sharing, giving, and connecting people. But at what cost?

Many times we work so hard to be good that we don't know who we really are. We as women often get caught up defining ourselves by who we are to others: a good mother or a great wife. But who are you without the titles and the measure of good or bad?

I believe these thought processes are ingrained in us as children. Good brings rewards and praise, but good should not be equated with value. Good can be represented as our choices, but not as a measure of who we are. Let me give you another example:

I was taking my daughter to class one week and heard another parent reprimanding her daughter for constant negative reports from the teacher. I believe in discipline; however, the message that was being ingrained in the child made me pause. She said to her daughter, "No kisses for you today, Abby. Mommy doesn't kiss bad girls." While the intent was coming from a good place, her daughter at the age of four was heartbroken. She burst into tears and begged for a hug and a kiss.

Abby had not gotten in trouble yet, but her mother wanted a good report for the day before she would embrace her child. Imagine how confusing this could be to a four year old. Love was now conditional based on her ability to get a good report every day. Imagine if the mother had said, "I still love you, Abby. Now make me proud and have a good day." This would have let Abby know that her mother would not waiver on her behavior, but still loved her. Now Abby could grow up thinking it is normal for someone to reject you unless you do what they want you to do. Abby could potentially become a pleaser to get constant validation and affirmation. Yet we wonder where these habits begin!

Many of us form our self-image around how others see us as children until we decide to become the image we hold within. Some people are angry. I was angry. This was because I always knew there were more options, a healthier way to communicate and deal with frustrations, and a better way of life for those willing to create it. But it's easy to get stuck when we don't know where to begin. We think maybe it's by being good and doing right. Maybe by being responsible and taking our roles seriously, we will get the life we envisioned.

For most of us, this is not enough. It takes work. During my pause, I reached a point where I needed to commit to myself to become whole. Whole from the inside out. Whole without the lingering of the past. Whole without others' perceptions or limitations or judgments of what I should or should not be. Whole in terms of the full potential that burned inside of me.

I want that for you, too, but only you know what that image looks like. Where do we begin? When you feel like you are doing all that you can and striving to be your best, but nothing will give, you must pause. This is also a surrender.

During my pause I experienced this with one of the most important relationships in my life. It was time to surrender my way of thinking, the pain of the past, and walking on eggshells with every conversation. It was time to get help. For us this meant a counseling session to face the pain head on. My life completely shifted in that moment. It's like every dark cloud in the sky parted ways and the light beamed on my face. I was facing the hard topics head-on and giving people back their baggage while taking account for my own.

Sometimes communication is the only way to get to the root of the pain. Some memories are so painful or were created so long ago that we don't realize that they grow just like an invisible weed in a garden that will spread and eventually hurt the other produce in our lives. Please be bold and courageous enough to check every vulnerable corner of your mind, body, and heart to make sure you have faced head on those painful moments of the past.

The pain I had inside ran so deep that the memory had broken trust. When trust is broken, especially as a child, you form a protective shell. This protective shell would later become the eggshells that would invisibly appear during every conversation. Once everything was put out into the open, it's like they were swept into the garbage where they belonged. It was scary and painful, but so worth it. I learned that we must give others, even those who have added to our pain, the same compassion and forgiveness that we seek.

It's important that we get to know who we are and embrace it. No one is perfect. Every single person has traits that they love and others that they wish they could change. When we are bold enough to take our own life and see it for what it is, a newfound power resonates within us. It's like putting all the cards on the table. Some you like. Some you don't. When you can face what you don't like from a perspective of gratitude with the courage to change it or forgive, then you are led to what the next step should look like. Most people choose to stay stuck at the current place, always focusing on what has gone wrong. Or they want to remind you of your past. But guess what? You can take your power back and fly.

I decided to surrender. I had to then forgive. Once I did, I realized that people had also forgiven me. People had accepted me as less than perfect. People had been patient with me. We must be patient with others.

Now that I am a parent, hopefully I will do a good job and my children will understand that I did my best. When we place ourselves in others' shoes for a moment, it is easier to show compassion. This is not a microwave process. So many times, I hear people say, "Oh, Girl! I let that go," or "I've moved on." The truth is, very few people are bold enough to sit in the pain long enough to fully process it, get the lesson, and release it. It has taken years of wanting to align with my whole self and my purpose to get to this chapter. We are all a steady work in progress, but the inner work and commitment is worth it. You are worth it. Get your fight back and get what you deserve.

◆◆◆

INVICTUS

by **William Ernest Henley**

Out of the night that covers me,
Black as the pit from pole to pole,
I thank whatever gods may be
For my unconquerable soul.

In the fell clutch of circumstance
I have not winced nor cried aloud.
Under the bludgeonings of chance
My head is bloody, but unbowed.

Beyond this place of wrath and tears
Looms but the Horror of the shade,
And yet the menace of the years
Finds and shall find me unafraid.

It matters not how strait the gate,
How charged with punishments the scroll,
I am the master of my fate,
I am the captain of my soul.

Pause #11

Take this time to pause and examine your thoughts.

List your most painful memories.

List the people involved.

How do you feel writing this?

Have your truly forgiven?

If you could write a letter to each person, what would it say? Don't filter it to be nice. Just empty your heart.

An extended pause nurtures and supports a transformation. Think of a caterpillar. After they hatch, they enter a period of growth. They shed their skin four or more times to keep up with this rapid process. Even before entering their cocoon, they spend their time in preparation, making sure that they have received enough nutrients to endure this stage of metamorphosis.[10]

---

[10] "Life Cycle - Flight of the Butterflies." *Flight of the Butterflies*. Web. <http://www.flightofthebutterflies.com/life-cycle/>.

The caterpillar reaches a point in life where it must embrace an intentional pause. If not, it will never grow from its cocoon. The caterpillar doesn't just stop for a quick break. It understands that it must step into the shadows to embrace the growth process.

Just before the caterpillar emerges as a butterfly, the outer covering of the cocoon becomes completely transparent. All the inner fluids swell up until it can no longer remain confined in its current environment.

How often do we outgrow where we are? Our past is critical to our foundation and development, but it is natural to outgrow certain things. The butterfly is now able to fly, where it once crawled confined to the ground. The butterfly has a new purpose in life; it now pollenates the flowers. Each butterfly is unique with it's own combination of beautiful colors like you and me.

Pause #12

Can you think of a particular period in your life that seemed like that of a caterpillar?

What about the cocoon? Have you ever embraced a positive period of self-discovery?

Did you emerge as a new or transformed person?

How would you describe your colors?

We'd love to celebrate with you. Please post your answers at *www.tierradestinyreid.com*.

◆ ◆ ◆

EMERGE

by Tierra Destiny Reid

It's almost time,
You've done your role.
Slow down your pace,
Listen to your soul.
Your time has come.
It won't be long.
Hear your heart,
Sing your song.
Embrace the change, your time has come.
It may be lonely, you may miss fun.
It's okay my love,
Because you are leaving the past.
You must embrace your growth,
Life ends too fast.

TWELVE
Things to Remember

All of this may sound easy. It may sound like I've mastered it, but the reality is no one has mastered it. It's life. Life is a journey. What I do know is that I have taken the time to enjoy a nice long beautiful pause in many areas of my life to prioritize and gain clarity in others. Even while writing this book, major changes occurred in my life before I could publish it. The tips below helped me flow with grace. I've also learned some valuable lessons along the way. These are just a few tips to help you during this critical moment in your journey:

- Take Your Time
- Don't Become Complacent
- No Speeding Out of a Pause

- Stay Positive
- Be Confident

Take Your Time

As I began to reflect and think on a higher level, I was able to explore myself on a deeper level. I realized that doing the work takes time. You cannot rush the process. According to the Oxford English Dictionary, a **process** is defined as **a series of actions or steps taken in order to achieve a particular end**. Think of something that you want to use, but it has been left in the garage for years. It may have gotten dirty, rusted, or even mildewed. You can't just rinse it off and think it will be clean. It may take cleaning it, letting it dry, and cleaning it again until you reach the goal. So many times we give up just before that last wash. Don't rush and don't give up. You must embrace this time.

Don't Become Complacent

Stopping your routine for too long may lead to complacency. Bringing everything to a complete halt can sometimes work against you during this process. Continue to do things you enjoy such as reading or yoga. My pause showed me how much I loved the things I was already doing and how much I was meant to continue doing the things I began. But there were also things I needed to get in order in my life. I focused especially on doing things in moderation.

111

No Speeding Out of a Pause

Be careful not to hit the gas out of your pause. Again, it's all about finding moderation. Once you discover what the new direction for your life is, ease out of your pause. Walk into your next season relaxed and geared up to bloom. Think about how long it takes a flower to grow. You will not get a tulip overnight. Plant seeds during your pause, be patient, and prepare for the harvest.

"Sometimes we need disappointments to remind us of why we are shooting for something bigger and better. Sometimes new forms of rejection are signs of growing on a new level. It comes with the climb. You are building new muscle."

Stay Positive

You may have insecurities, but it's important that you reach a point where you can casually admit those things that you struggle with. We all experience this. Sometimes we allow other people's advice, judgment, side eyes, love, or attitudes to keep things to ourselves.

I learned over time that it's best to share your feelings, but discern who to share with. If you surround yourself with negative thinkers, of course, you won't feel comfortable sharing, but as you meet positive, healthy thinkers, you can open up and celebrate your weaknesses and be okay.

Coming to terms with these issues actually gives us more power and inner strength. There's no need to hide them because we have all been there a time or two. The insecurity may just become something you simply don't like, but now it's not a toxin floating around in your mind that begins to affect everything around you. Stay positive.

Be Confident

Confidence is something that people say you either have or you don't. I believe that it can also come and go during different seasons of our journey. Our levels of confidence and self-esteem provide a gauge for our strengths and needs, letting us know that we are comfortable in some areas and may need work in others.[11] Of course, most people have something that they are working on or wish they could improve. We are all human.

Confidence is an inner knowing and contentment that has nothing to do with the ego. Real confidence is strictly internal and is not measured by external factors

---

[11] Casriel, Erika. "Confidence: Stepping Out." *Psychology Today*. 1 Mar. 2007. Web.
<http://www.psychologytoday.com/articles/200702/confidence-stepping-out>.

or changes. Confidence can come from the quietest person in the room or the most powerful speaker of influence who is passionate about his or her cause.

It takes true confidence to face disappointment, rejection, abandonments, or failure and know that it does not define you. *It only refines you.* Keep going!

"Never wish for someone else's shoes. You never know the size, the comfort level, what they're made of, or the distance you must go in them. Celebrate YOU! You look good in your shoes."

THIRTEEN
*Things Look Different From a Distance
Than They Do Close Up*

We often give up on our dreams due to lack of confidence and feelings of having inadequate skills.[12] I want you to know that just because something didn't work the first time, doesn't mean it never will. Exposure to new places, people, and cultures seems to nurture this perspective. There are millions of opportunities and options in this world. The buck never stops with one situation. *Do the best you can with what you have now.* This is something I tell myself as

[12] Semple, Stuart. "Don't Give Up on Your Creative Dreams." *The Guardian.* Guardian News and Media, 25 Feb. 2013. Web.
<http://www.theguardian.com/culture-professionals-network/culture-professionals-blog/2013/feb/25/young-creatives-dream-career>.

well as others. You have exactly what you need right now to do what you are meant to be doing right now.

I recently had a project. I was so focused on the plan as written and the contractors as selected that I completely forgot about the handful of support I had from years ago. We ran into a situation where we needed additional support, but it would have been better if it were someone who already knew the brand, understood what was needed, and was aligned with my core values.

Once I stopped being frustrated about the time delays, changes that would need to happen, and the loss of production, I was able to focus on a solution. I realized I had more than enough options. When I really let go of all the negative energy, two friends from the past contacted me that were actually in the field of production that I needed to add. Sometimes it takes us stepping back to analyze the full picture before everything comes together.

"As you become your best, you will only accept the best from those around you!"

Surroundings

Something that helps me keep going and moving forward is surrounding myself with positive people and constantly thinking of my blessings and things to be grateful for. I have a loving family, friends, supporters; and endless memories, talents, and responsibilities that remind me that life is bigger than me. I am a contributor to life. We all experience it differently. How we experience life is dependent upon our approach and thought process. When I find myself being frustrated or overwhelmed with something, I try to remind myself that my contribution may not be healthy and that it is my responsibility to change it.

You probably never think twice about the power that lies in what you see, read, and hear. Once I realized how powerful this was, I started paying close attention to it. Even as we observe certain behaviors, our brains interpret them as if we are performing the actions ourselves.[13] Filling our surroundings with things that are positive allows us to put positive things back out into the world.

During my pause, I created my first gratitude board. Instead of success or forward vision, I included the things I was grateful for. I love to write. I have countless journals all over the place with a few pages filled in each, yellow legal pads with thoughts jotted down, and binders with pages of poetry. Writing is very therapeutic and a release process for me. That is

---

[13] Pillay, Srinivasan. "Is There Scientific Evidence for the "Law of Attraction"?" *The Huffington Post*. TheHuffingtonPost.com, 17 Mar. 2009. Web. <http://www.huffingtonpost.com/srinivasan-pillay/is-there-scientific-evide_b_175189.html>.

how I channel my ideas, pain, or clear my mind. I realized within the last few years that creating visuals provided the consistency for me that journaling did not, however. I like that they are not all chronologically streamlined and that I can reflect on them at any given moment.

The visual gratitude board is great. I can add pictures, magazine clippings, or keepsakes with a thumbtack and keep moving. I also love word clouds because words are powerful. You can create your own like the one here at www.wordle.net.

Perspective

Embracing the process does not mean it will be peaches and cream. It does not mean you won't want to stop and jump back into the rush of life before you truly do the work necessary in this phase or enjoy the comfort of the things that feel natural to you. You will have those thoughts, but if you truly believe that there is more to life than what you have achieved so far without releasing the pain, then you must keep doing the work.

This may mean eliminating outside phone calls or diving into more reading for an extended period of time. Travel, explore new surroundings, and try things you have never done. When we reach for the same people, places, and things, we are repeating the cycle.

To be honest, during my pause I realized how much I am attached to certain foods. Although that did not completely disappear, it gave me an inner power to make a conscious decision and not make an excuse. Now I actually think about my choices and accept when I am making a preference instead of unconsciously filling a void. I was able to see what my pattern was and decided to face it head on. Some things take a lifetime to discover. The first step is becoming aware and admitting that you want a change.

Courage

I am not sure if it takes more courage to begin or to keep going. Both beginning and continuing are dynamic decisions that require strength, courage, and vulnerability either way.

To begin means to do something you have never done. There is no manual, no rules, no safety zone, no guarantee. It is a true leap. It is making a decision without a defined destination, yet the desire in your heart and the thoughts in your mind tell you it's right. It feels right. Your spirit is aligned. It's the ultimate act of faith.

Quite naturally as a social cause entrepreneur, I have a deep admiration for those on this path because we dedicate our time to create change in the world without guarantees and without a roadmap. We take the hits to create something bigger and better to hopefully make a difference for someone else. Any crossroads or major life-changing decisions take a mixture of courage, confidence, truth, and determination.

On the other hand, the courage to keep going means that you have more than likely taken a number of hits and have been given a million reasons to quit, but have somehow mustered up the strength to get back up. What about the times when you have no strength left? What about when things don't work as planned or you are rejected? What would make someone keep going versus throwing in the towel? Faith. Faith that this is a season of preparation for what is to come and that also takes courage, strength, determination and an inner confidence that is not led by the ego, but by the heart and spirit.

Pause #13

How do you show up and what do you add when you are involved?

How do people feel after being around you?

What do you contribute to the lives of others who share experiences with you?

There was even a moment of guilt for the achievement and success. I later realized that this came from needing that time to reflect and know that each of us deserve the rewards that come our way.

-Tierra Destiny

FOURTEEN

Flying Without Limits: Grab Your Carry-On

There is an inner struggle and frustration that many of us feel– a feeling of having greater power and potential, but never actualizing it. Some of us will continue the cycles of our past, while others will get stuck never fully embracing who we are and who we were created to be.

After pouring out to hundreds of women and children with all that I had inside, traveling across the country, and empowering the customers in my store, it was time that I stop and celebrate the journey. I had to celebrate all the hard work and all the beautiful experiences that had taken place. If not, they would have come and gone in the blink of an eye and been a distant memory in my brain. But thanks to a powerful conscious pause, I was able to not only reflect on the beauty of this last chapter, but also really reflect on the lessons, conversations, and growth that had taken place.

As the signs kept showing up to slow down, I decided to listen. If not, instead of selling my store, I could have lost it. Instead of taking advantage of the chance to think, reflect, and prioritize, I could have crashed, broken down, and gotten sick. It's hard to make yourself pause, but so worth it in the end.

If we don't get the lesson the first time, it will show up again. If we don't get it the second time, it comes back around. A third time, you know the story. It's not going anywhere until we get it.

Yes, I looked great and felt very joyous doing all the things I loved, but there were never weeks of true rest and reflection, unless I was on vacation. It is so important that we take personal retreats to reflect, and even more important that we allow ourselves to truly embrace the chapter that we are in. There are times when we do need to push because we are in a heavy execution phase, but there are times when we pause and celebrate what has been experienced, rest, and gear up for our next mission on the journey. We must protect ourselves and be willing to live in alignment with our purpose, moving closer to it with each step.

"Being tired is a sign. It's best to listen to your body. This means your work is complete for this chapter. Think of a runner. Races require you to train, run, and then rest."

Celebrate with Gratitude

It is so important for us to celebrate small successes. It's easy for us to stay focused on our huge goals, dreams, or overall mission and purpose. It is just as important to know that baby steps are leading us there and we are one step closer than we were before. The people you encounter along the way are able to witness your transformation and be inspired. Each of us moving forward inspires everyone around us to do the same. Celebrate the decision to try. The effort to do the work. The courage it takes to pause. The love it takes to want more from yourself and reach your highest potential. That is a beautiful thing and it helps all of us.

Have you ever seen someone going after their dreams and finally make it? There's nothing like it! I cry when I see athletes win a big game or an Olympian win a medal because these are real life examples of people who have trained and done the work over and over again until they were strong enough, wise enough, and prepared enough to reach that ultimate goal. We are the same. We cannot give up, but we must be willing to do the work to grow into the person that is ready to live and handle whatever our dreams may be.

"I could've never imagined the freedom I have.... My life has completely changed for the better! I am free from the limitations that I had unconsciously placed on myself. I am who I am...completely free from the life that was holding me back from being the person I was meant to be."

- Stephanie Lynn Campbell

Dream New Dreams

2012 was a dream come true explosion on every level for me. Personal, professional, spiritual, you name it. I never really thought it was possible to outgrow your dreams. It felt weird and a little overwhelming. There was even a moment of guilt for the achievement and success. I later realized that this came from needing that time to reflect and know that each of us deserves the rewards that come our way.

When you want the same thing for all of those around you, it can be hard to embrace where you are. You may want to help, but being in a healthy place will allow you to create ways to help without depleting yourself in the process. Pausing allowed me to begin dreaming new dreams. These were dreams beyond me, my family, and what I wanted out of this life. These were dreams that would impact the lives of those who may never know me. Dreams that could somehow make life better for others and help share the gifts that had been given to me.

When you reach a point where you must dream new dreams, you begin to realize that anything is truly possible. There is a level of accountability that comes over your life and you understand that it was never really about you to begin with.

Your life is a gift and an instrument to help the driving purpose and overall missions of God. We each have a gift, a purpose, a role in progression and growth. Understanding that our existence matters and that even the smallest acts of kindness can brighten someone's day and remind them that there is still love and light in the world, is a huge deal. A genuine smile, a phone call, a card, and conversation from the heart: these are the moments that matter. It's not about the accolades and public recognition. It's a combination of all the private exchanges of love that keep us going as well.

Although you may not see where your existence is inspiring someone to keep going, it is. That is why you must keep moving forward. There is so much waiting for you. We need you to keep going because you matter.

Keep Going

So many women have asked me how I keep going and where I get my strength and endurance. Well, to be honest, when I was younger and struggled with processing disappointments and stressful situations, I would think about my future a lot. Options. Freedom. Creating the environment that was inspiring. I started to tap into that inner light that reminds us that if we can just keep going, there is a brighter day.

My mother has tremendous strength and persistence, so these traits were embedded in me. Even when I thought about giving up, it was just too scary. I reminded myself that God loves me too much. Where would I go? I had too much to lose.

Life can be very confusing and stressful for us as children, but I soon found out that it could be the same as an adult. The difference as an adult is you have the choice of whom you live with and whom you spend your time around. So as a child, I just reminded myself that "adults" could do whatever they want. I just had to keep going until I could take care of myself. I laugh at that thought now because a whole lot of work and accountability comes with that, but I am filled with gratitude as I reflect on the love of God that was instilled in me as a child. I didn't realize the power and magnitude of that at the time. I am now grateful for my mother's strength to keep going. Her ambition is unmatched.

My mother, although struggling as a single parent for many years without transportation, would make our spiritual foundation a priority. I remember many times riding the bus to church. The spirit lives within. That is what was carrying me— the ability to tune and channel within and block out everything around me.

As an adult it is very similar, but there are still different things that support this practice. The process of meditation has been a great help recently to train and quiet my mind, but even before I was introduced to the formal process and practice, I was training my mind to think positive, think bigger, broader, and know that this world is bigger than me and my situation. It is bigger than any problem that I could ever have and we are all here for a reason.

I love airplanes! I mean absolutely love them. Just as I do eagles. I am always looking up. I seldom look down when I am walking. In much the same way, I have always found peace and contentment in a big view. Life is many combinations of many things coming together at just the right time. Things are somehow always working together to help you, but you must do your part.

Believe in Yourself

No matter how many times you must start over, it is important that you believe in yourself to get back up and move forward. So many times we focus on the distance from the destination and forget to celebrate the fact that we were willing to start over. Willing to face the fear. Willing to get back up and see if we could make it even a little bit farther this time. You can and you will because you decided to.

When you believe in yourself, there is nothing that can really come in your way. The mind is so powerful. We can build and create whatever it is we envision. So keep going. Go hard. Get focused and be unapologetic about your commitment to striving to be your best self. People will always have opinions about what you could have done better or done differently, but what matters most is that you are willing to do something. Done is better than perfect. Keep checking off your dreams. We need your gifts.

Conscious Living

The ability to move toward a specific set of goals not only takes courage and discipline, but also determination and a conscious decision to stay on track no matter how many curve balls are thrown your way. Anyone can say they want to keep moving forward and want this or that out of life, but how many people will not accept anything less than giving what it takes?

Life happens to all of us every single day. Storms come. Disappointments and frustrations come, but these are not reasons to give up. Never stop pushing.

Don't allow yourself to just sit focusing on what went wrong. What progress comes out of that?

It's all about perspective. When you decide what you will think about, what you will work towards, and what difference you want to make in this world, it begins to happen. So make a conscious decision today and do it.

Our greatest gift to the world is to look at our present, embrace it, and decide who we want to become.

Shine Bright... Unapologetically

-Tierra Destiny

FIFTEEN
Already Amazing

While life may occasionally feel hectic and overwhelming, the real work will happen during the pause. Ruth Kaiser sent me a message during my pause that said *The hardest thing you'll ever do will become the most important thing you've ever done.* Those words alone gave me peace. The real work happened during the pause because I spent time searching and self-reflecting.

Only we know the things about ourselves that need correcting. We sometimes hold ourselves to unrealistic standards when we should be celebrating who we are and where we are with our flaws, dysfunctions, and mishaps.

What's mind-blowing is that even after all the work, all the sweat, the tears, the questions, the answers, the journaling, the reading, the life classes, the walks in the park, the chats with girlfriends, the chats with mom, the prayers, the meditation; even after all that, I came back around to my simple truth: *we are already amazing!*

It's all part of the process. The energy we spend questioning the process could be used embracing and flowing through it. But a pause allows us to tap into our inner power and see a clear reflection of our reality, a beautiful picture at our here, our now, our today, our present. Our greatest gift to the world is to look at our present, embrace it, and decide who we want to become.

My message and hope for you and myself is that we begin to believe, understand, and never forget that we are amazing. Yes. Already amazing. What we will discover during our pause is that most of the baggage, pain, confusion, disappointments, and strain is associated with other people, our past, and experiences that are now over and done with.

These outside conditions do not define us. We must tap into our inner strength, our inner power and fight for it! When I say fight I do not mean fight others, debate, and shout out loud to the world with titles and accomplishments. I mean fight any negative thought, feeling, and belief that tries to hinder you and hold you back. This is important because your obedience, authentic release, and sharing your gift and inner power is directly connected to someone else's destiny.

When you truly embrace that you are amazing, you will no longer search for it, seek it from others, or compromise your greatness in the same way. Our questions change. Our focus changes. We begin asking and wondering how we can use more of it for our purpose and we achieve healthy fulfillment when we tap into this power that comes with the pause.

COMMITMENT TO YOURSELF

Today I commit to

_____

and nothing that happens will ever stop me from
pursuing _____.
No matter how hard or unpredictable my situation, I
know that because I have decided to
_____, things or situations may
show up in my life to prepare me for achieving my
goals so that I may serve that role in the best possible
state of being.

LETTER FROM THE AUTHOR

Hello There,

I want to take a moment to say thank you. Thank you for reading this book and sharing your time with me. Thank you for supporting me and the movement to inspire others. Thank you for caring enough about your journey to reach out and discover something new. I love that. I am the same way. When something intrigues me, I like to explore. It is my hope that something that was shared in this book will inspire you to ask yourself a question that leads to a new answer or makes you stop and pause for a moment. I hope that you will embrace who you are and where you have been, and begin to build upon your heart's greatest desires. You are beautiful and I don't even know you. I believe everyone has some form of light within. We are children of God. The fact that you have finished this book, says so much about you. I can't tell you how many books I have actually skimmed through, just hoping to grab a quick nugget or two, but not you. You finished and I want to thank you for becoming a part of my journey.
Please take a moment to join me and others worldwide as we share our stories and support each other, reaching deeper within. I would love to hear from you. I read every single comment. I really do! I'll be waiting for your feedback.

Continued blessings to you!

Love,
Tierra Destiny

I WANT TO HEAR FROM YOU

Let's Connect!

Step 1:
Visit www.tierradestinyreid.com and sign up for our free newsletter to keep up with the latest events, updates, and fun surprises

Step 2:
Leave your feedback on our guestbook. How do you know when to *pause*? I want to hear from you.

Step 3:
Help us spread the word. Please suggest the book to a friend who may need it and encourage them to join the movement.

Join the conversation.
Use #PausingwithTDR to join the movement

For speaking engagements and media inquiries:

e-mail inquiries@tierradestinyreid.com

TDR Brands International
2221 Peachtree Rd. NE D249
Atlanta, GA 30309

SPECIAL THANKS

I'd like to give a special thanks to all the women who contributed to this work. Without your courage and willingness to share your stories, this book would be incomplete.

Amandeep Kaur
Angela Stalcup
Annelle Johnson Elder
Connie Phillips-Gilbert
Cynthia D. King
Delmar Johnson
Eardie M. Houston
Felicia Joy
Joy McLaughlin
Kaira Akita
Lisa 'L.A.' Matthews
Lorea M. Sample
Rhonda Glaze
S. Press
Stephanie Lynn Campbell
Ursula Harrington

OVER 40 TOPICS OF DISCUSSION

MEET THE AUTHOR

Tierra Destiny Reid is a wife; grateful mother of two; and an innovative trailblazer in retail, entrepreneurship, and women's empowerment. The author of the revolutionary empowerment guide *The Power of Peace in a Pause*, Tierra is passionate about using her life lessons and gifts to inspire women around the world to pause and propel their way to authentic success, leadership, and service.

Known for her unique mix of heart, accountability, and hard-driving business savvy, Tierra is the President of TDR Brands International and the visionary behind The Retail Campus, an emerging global resource for women with startup retail products and storefronts. Her unconventional and inspirational approach has made her a sought out speaker and contributor for female-focused brands including Tory Johnson's Spark & Hustle, Little Pink Book, WISE Symposium, Blogalicious, and the National Association of Resale and Thrift Stores 25th Anniversary Conference. She has been featured on Good Morning America Work Spot, Success Magazine, FOX, and CBS. Tierra is a proud Oprah Winfrey Network Ambassador who attributes her resiliency to her mother who raised her alone for several years. For this reason, TDR dreams of creating a nonprofit for single mothers striving to also blaze trails while becoming their best selves along the way. She witnessed first hand how critical peace can be in the midst of a storm and wants to share tools and techniques with others who are doing the best they can with what they have.

Visit her online at www.tierradestinyreid.com.

REFERENCES

Casriel, Erika. "Confidence: Stepping Out." *Psychology Today*. 1 Mar. 2007. Web.
<http://www.psychologytoday.com/articles/200702/confidence-stepping-out>.

"Exercise for Stress and Anxiety." *Anxiety and Depression Association of America*. Web.
<http://www.adaa.org/living-with-anxiety/managing-anxiety/exercise-stress-and-anxiety>.

Goldring, Clarann. "Forgiveness."*Common Sense Psychology Website*.Web.
<http://www.commonsensepsychology.com/forgiveness.php>.

Henley, William Ernest. "Invictus." *Poetry Foundation*. Poetry Foundation, n.d. Web.

"How to Hit the Reset Button After Losing Your Dream Job - Oprah's Lifeclass – OWN."<https://www.youtube.com/watch?v=2G7Ds4NgSng>.

Huffington, Christina. "Single Motherhood Increases Dramatically For Certain Demographics, Census Bureau Reports." *The Huffington Post*. TheHuffingtonPost.com, 1 May 2013. Web.

<http://www.huffingtonpost.com/2013/05/01/single
-motherhood-increases-census-
report_n_3195455.html>.

Lally, Phillippa, Cornelia H. M. Van Jaarsveld, Henry
W. W. Potts, and Jane Wardle. "How Are Habits
Formed: Modelling Habit Formation In The Real
World." *European Journal of Social Psychology* 40.6 (2010):
998-1009. Print.

"Life Cycle - Flight of the Butterflies." *Flight of the
Butterflies.*Web.<http://www.flightofthebutterflies.co
m/life-cycle/>.

Pillay, Srinivasan. "Is There Scientific Evidence for the
"Law of Attraction"?" *The Huffington Post.*
TheHuffingtonPost.com, 17 Mar. 2009. Web.
<http://www.huffingtonpost.com/srinivasan-
pillay/is-there-scientific-evide_b_175189.html>.

Semple, Stuart. "Don't Give Up on Your Creative
Dreams." *The Guardian.* Guardian News and Media, 25
Feb. 2013. Web.
<http://www.theguardian.com/culture-professionals-
network/culture-professionals-
blog/2013/feb/25/young-creatives-dream-career>.

Shriver, Maria. "The Power of the Pause." *Maria
Shriver-Powered by Inspiration.* MOS Enterprises, 12 May
2012. Web.
<http://mariashriver.com/blog/2012/05/power-of-
the-pause-maria-shriver-commencement-address/>.

Sifferlin, Alexandra. "How People-Pleasing May Lead to Overeating." *Time*. Time. Web. <http://healthland.time.com/2012/02/02/how-people-pleasing-leads-to-overeating/>.

Singer, Michael A. *The Untethered Soul: The Journey Beyond Yourself*. Oakland, CA: New Harbinger Publications, 2007. Print.

Williamson, Marianne. *A Return to Love: Reflections on the Principles of a Course in Miracles*. New York, NY: Harper Collins, 1992. Print.

Made in the USA
Charleston, SC
16 December 2014